SIR WALTER RALEGH
AND THE
QUEST FOR EL DORADO

Sir Walter Ralegh

AND THE

Quest for El Dorado

MARC ARONSON

CLARION BOOKS ▪ NEW YORK

Clarion Books
a Houghton Mifflin Company imprint
215 Park Avenue South, New York, NY 10003
Copyright © 2000 Marc Aronson

The text for this book was set in 14-point Fournier.

Book design by Trish Parcell Watts
Maps on pages xii-xiii, 71, and 130 by Kayley LeFaiver.

For information about permission to reproduce selections from this book,
write to Permissions, Houghton Mifflin Company,
215 Park Avenue South, New York, NY 10003.

Printed in China

Library of Congress Cataloging-in-Publication Data

Aronson, Marc.
Sir Walter Ralegh and the quest for El Dorado / by Marc Aronson.
p. cm
Includes bibliographical references and index.
Summary: Recounts the adventurous life of the English explorer
and courtier who spelled his name "Ralegh" and led many expeditions
to the New World.
ISBN 0-395-84827-X
1. Ralegh, Walter, Sir, 1554?–1618—Juvenile literature.   2. Great
Britain—Court and courtiers—Biography—Juvenile literature.
3. Guiana—Discovery and exploration—Juvenile literature.
4. Explorers—England—Biography—Juvenile literature.
[1. Raleigh, Walter, Sir, 1554?–1618.   2. Explorers.]   I. Title.
DA86.22.R2   A76   2000
942.055092—dc21
[B]   99-043096

LEO 10 9 8 7 6 5 4
4500413051

To the next generation of explorers:
Cordelia and Clare, Kabir and Anisha, Juliet and Peter,
and all those to come

Contents

Acknowledgments

This book is a product of Dorothy Briley's vision; I only wish she could have lived to see it become a reality.

Two people were instrumental in making this text into a book, and two others played key roles in photo research. Thanks to Margaret Santangelo for doing the spadework in getting photos, and to Jim Batten for research leads and support via E-mail from Devon. My wife, Marina Budhos, inspired me to put on paper the cinematic sweep I saw in Ralegh's life and insisted that I make every word count. Virginia Buckley's sensitive and firm editing made all the difference in turning this into a book for the readers I wanted to reach. I learned a great deal from her. Thanks also to Renée Cafiero and Jennifer Greene for sensitive fine-tuning.

I am grateful to Alex and Maricel Presilla for providing a country home in which one key chapter was written, and to my mother, Lisa Aronson, for constant support and encouragement. Amy Johnson told me the book read well, which almost made it true.

Note to Readers

Sir Walter Ralegh's name is most often spelled Raleigh in America, but all scholars agree that Ralegh is how he wrote it during his adult life. I have followed that usage. But when quoting from prose and poetry of his day, I have sometimes chosen to modernize spellings that create unnecessary confusion. Sir Walter's family name was pronounced RAW-lie, or RAW-lee, as is suggested by this word puzzle a lawyer named John Manningham posed. The challenge was to guess the name from the description:

> *The foe to the stomach, and the word of disgrace*
> *Shows the gentleman's name with bold face.*

The answer was raw lie, Sir Walter himself.

The notes section in back offers complete bibliographic information for every quotation and for every important source used in this book. Rather than use footnotes, I have listed the notes in the order of the text. Those interested in more detailed discussions of historical debates, as well as parallels between some of the events in this book and examples from other times and places, should also consult the notes section. The more I worked on this book, the more fascinated I became with Ralegh and his age. Many other writers have felt similarly about the period, which means there are many wonderful books awaiting your discovery.

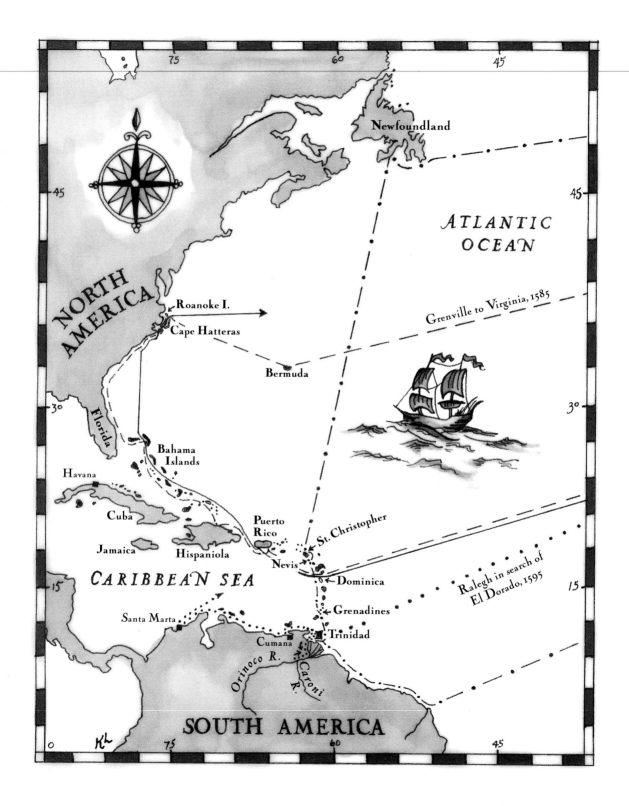

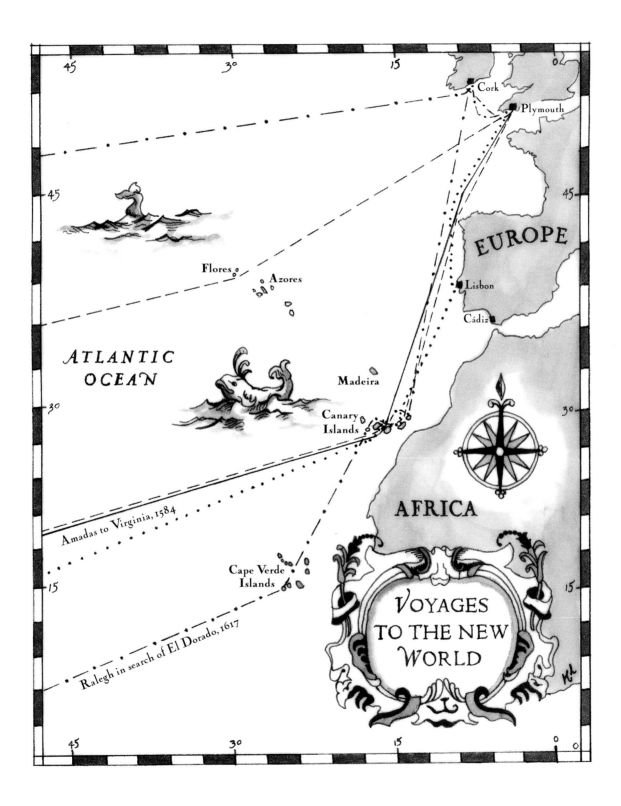

45   30   15   0

Cork

Plymouth

45

EUROPE

Flores

Azores

Lisbon

Cádiz

45

ATLANTIC
OCEAN

30

Madeira

Canary
Islands

30

Amadas to Virginia, 1584

AFRICA

15

Cape Verde
Islands

VOYAGES
TO THE NEW
WORLD

15

Ralegh in search of El Dorado, 1617

45   30   15   0

BETWEEN PARADISE AND THE
SERPENT'S MOUTH

It is June of 1595, and Sir Walter Ralegh is trapped on the northern coast of South America. Behind him surges the mighty Orinoco River, gateway to paradise. Ahead of him looms the dark sea. He is in "a most desperate state." Almost one hundred years before, in the very same place, Christopher Columbus had been terrified by "an awful roaring," the sound of that immense river emptying into the sea. Columbus decided that the river must run from Eden itself, for he had "never either read or heard of fresh water coming in so large a quantity" so close to the ocean. A century of conquest had caused Europeans to lower their sights. Ralegh did not sail to the New World in search of Eden. His goal was the golden city of El Dorado.

Deep in the jungle, Ralegh and his crew thought they had nearly reached the fabled city. It lay just five more days ahead, a wise old chief assured them. But Ralegh had neither the manpower nor the strength to push on and find it. Then came the crisis. Once his crew turned their small barges to go back down the river to their ships, the land seemed to close up on them. Terrible thunderstorms drenched the bedraggled explorers and forced them to take a new route through the trackless tangle of streams and rivulets that is the Orinoco Delta. Now they were at the coast, at night, and an even more mighty and terrifying storm broke around them.

Should they risk plunging across the choppy waters sailors called the Serpent's Mouth? If they made it, they would reach the nearby island of Trinidad. Trinidad was a safe-enough landfall but occupied by the enemy, the Spanish. Or should they clamber onto their waiting galley, knowing it might not be able to sail in the shallow river mouth? Ralegh was "very doubtful which way to take," whether to "adventure in so great a billow, and in so doubtful weather, to cross the seas in my barge. The longer we tarried the worse it was."

After talking with his captains, Ralegh chose. At midnight, the crew "put ourselves in God's keeping, and thrust out into the sea." They arrived by morning, snuck up the island, and reached the rest of their ships. This was like so much of Ralegh's life: Chasing after glory, he plunged into a great adventure and came hauntingly close to dazzling success, only to have to flee for his life. In the end, he had nothing but courage, faith, and good sense, qualities that carried him through to the next impossible challenge.

Ralegh the adventurer hacking through uncharted jungle in search of the kingdom of gold; Ralegh the sea dog, sailing in speedy galleys to take Spanish treasure; Ralegh the careful thinker, who weighed evidence; Ralegh the great writer, whose account of this trip reads like an adventure story; Ralegh the man who relied only on himself; and Ralegh the man who always trusted in God—all of these were there on the edge of the South American continent.

This book tells the story of how he arrived seemingly so close to El Dorado, and what became of him after his dash across the cresting waves. For this entire journey was just one of Ralegh's many spectacular adventures. His life suited his era, when men could go off questing after dreams, and sometimes find them. To understand him we must understand those dreams, starting with the greatest of them all: El Dorado.

THE GOLDEN MAN

For nearly a century an international cast of characters—including Spanish noblemen and thieves, priests and soldiers, German merchants and Portuguese seamen, English knights and sailors, as well as squadrons of enslaved Africans and countless unfortunate South American natives—went on a quest. They marched through thousands upon thousands of miles of dense, insect-laden rain forest. They crawled up endless jagged slopes. Starving, they fought their way through seas of knife-sharp grass. All this to find El Dorado. Most were killed, or lost all their money, or contracted gruesome diseases. But did anyone find this golden land? Were the ceaseless rumors true? Was it there, hidden in the new continent, waiting to be conquered? That all depends on what El Dorado itself means.

Taken literally, El Dorado means "the Golden Man." In this sense, it refers to a story, perhaps first recorded in 1541, of a naked Chibcha king who was covered in gold. The Chibcha, also known as the Muiscas, were a native people who created a sophisticated civilization in what is now

Colombia. Some of their descendants can still be found there. The legendary Chibcha monarch was first greased with a sticky resin. Then gold was blown onto his body through mouth pipes similar to blowguns. Once his naked body was entirely clothed in gold, he would travel across a sacred lake in a raft and dip into the water, releasing the glittering paint. This did happen; it was true.

Lake Guatavita, in Colombia, may have been formed very recently by a meteorite. People could have seen the fiery ball fall from the sky, smashing

El Dorado being painted with a fine spray of gold, as imagined by a later European artist.
(FROM THE 1625 EDITION OF DE BRY'S *AMERICA*, BY PERMISSION OF THE BRITISH LIBRARY)

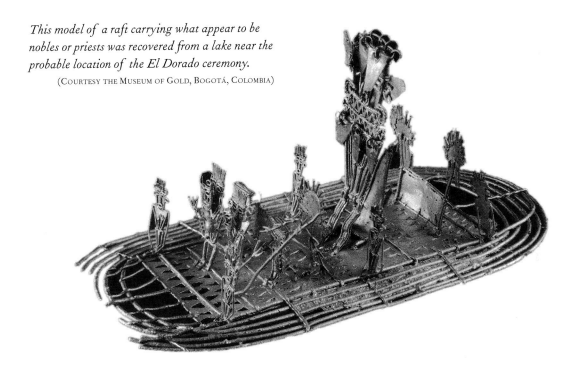

This model of a raft carrying what appear to be nobles or priests was recovered from a lake near the probable location of the El Dorado ceremony.
(COURTESY THE MUSEUM OF GOLD, BOGOTÁ, COLOMBIA)

into the ground to create the huge hole that became the lake. If they did, perhaps the terrifying event inspired them to send a king golden as the sun out onto the waters, to quiet the demon lurking in their depths. This is the legend the Spanish recorded, and that is what the miniature golden raft recovered from nearby Lake Siecha seems to depict: a golden king standing on a raft with his priests, setting out onto the lake.

The Chibcha probably stopped performing their golden ceremony even before the Spanish arrived. In this sense the entire enterprise was doomed. Nowhere on the continent could the conquistadors have found the radiant king they were seeking. No matter. The Europeans were looking not just for the king covered in gold but for the kingdom so rich that it could afford to use the precious ore as a sacred paint. El Dorado was the land of the Golden Man, the richest place on earth.

WHAT WAS EL DORADO?

In the sixteenth century, seeking a golden kingdom in what would later be called South America made sense. After all, in the early part of the century three had already been found, conquered, and looted: first the Aztec, by Hernando Cortés, in 1521; then the Inca, by Francisco Pizarro, in 1532; finally, the very Chibcha who had performed the golden man ceremony, by Gonzalo Jiménez de Quesada, in 1537. In each case Europeans had heard rumors of the kingdom and its great wealth long before they actually found it.

In the 1560s and 1570s Doradism—the yearning to find the next golden land—was whipped up by clever promoters and spread throughout Spain. Anyone with the tiniest bit of money to invest, or the chance to leave and join the latest expedition, did so with pleasure. One after another these efforts turned into dismal failures, yet nothing could dampen the mood of wild hope.

In 1569, at the age of seventy, Jiménez de Quesada set out once again into the jungle, only to return in total defeat three years later. This kind of mad search after a hopeless dream is called quixotic, after the title character in *Don Quixote*, the wonderful novel published by Miguel de Cervantes in 1605 (a second part came out in 1615). Appropriately enough, Jiménez de Quesada may have been one of the models Cervantes used in creating the

Man of La Mancha who quests after an impossible dream. Spain, and much of Europe, was in the grips of quixotic Doradism.

Not only was it hard for Europeans to judge fact from fable, it was difficult for them to see what they had already conquered. While there were tons of gold, silver, and gems waiting to be found in South America, these resources had to be extracted from the ground, not stolen from defeated kings and chiefs. In that sense, South America itself was a kind of El Dorado, a golden place to be exploited and mined.

When Columbus set out across the sea, he was seeking a trade route to the East, to the land of spices. But South America had many resources that were to be as valuable as the most precious Asian spices. Potatoes, tomatoes, corn, vanilla, and chilies, which did not exist outside the New World, are now worth far more than all the gold taken from defeated kingdoms. And cacao, which gives us chocolate, was for centuries a New World specialty. It replaced gold and silver and preceded oil as the South American bonanza. Once introduced from the Old World, coffee, sugarcane, cattle, and pigs flourished there. Though wealth did not come as quickly to planters as to conquistadors, South America did offer golden fortunes to those who found the right crop.

Few Europeans in these early days of conquest could see all this natural bounty as a kind of El Dorado. They had something very different in mind. Considering El Dorado as a kingdom to be conquered suggests a sudden and spectacular victory. That is the view of the winner, a glee only sharpened by the anguish of the defeated. Europe's golden dream was the native Americans' living nightmare.

That sense of triumph was a good part of the thrill of seeking El Dorado. Most of the conquistadors viewed the New World as a woman to

In this 1589 drawing showing Amerigo Vespucci discovering America, the new land is a naked woman, the Old World a fully clothed, educated man.

(COURTESY THE METROPOLITAN MUSEUM OF ART, GIFT OF THE ESTATE OF JAMES HAZEN HYDE, 1959)

be ravished. The poet John Donne, Ralegh's contemporary, made that clear in this poem to his mistress, though he was being more playful than the real conquerors:

> License my roving hands, and let them go
> Before, behind, between, above, below.
> O my America! My new-found-land,
> My kingdom safeliest when with one man mann'd.
> My mine of precious stones, my Emperie,
> How blest am I in discovering thee!

The soldiers felt a supreme joy in their mastery and the weakness or "primitiveness" of the natives. The plunder of kingdoms, the destruction of old gods, the enslavement of whole peoples were not merely successes; they were declarations of superiority. Patiently farming a crop just does not offer that kind of emotional thrill.

But the story does not end with greedy soldiers seeking new conquests. While many Europeans saw the New World as a place to affirm their mastery, others were not so sure. To these idealists, America's beautiful, unspoiled landscape and seemingly happy people suggested a chance for a new beginning. They did not believe that wise Christian Europeans were destined to rule this savage place. Rather, they hoped that poor, sinning people of the Old World would have a new chance across the sea to make better lives. The new land would bring a golden chance for a new and better way of living.

El Dorado could be a wild jungle full of glittering heathen statues that Christians would melt down and thus redeem. Or it could be a Garden of Eden, in which a new, more truly Christian person would be born. If the true Golden Land fit the first description, then the priests and protectors of the Indians who slowed the conquest deserved to be silenced. If the second were so, Adam's children were once again destroying Eden, and the slaughter could not stop soon enough.

Was there really an El Dorado in the New World? And if so, which one was it: the savage idols to steal, the fields to plow, or the garden of peace? It was Sir Walter Ralegh's fate to be the man who did the most to answer these questions. More than any other person, he tested and proved what the New World could be. Through him we can peer back to see the dreams the English brought with them to North America—the dreams that eventually gave birth to the United States. But to know those dreams, we must begin in England, not America, for it was in England that Ralegh's character was shaped.

Rising

Sir Walter Ralegh was one, that Fortune had picked . . .
to use as her Tennis-Ball, thereby to show what she could do;
for she tossed him up of nothing, and to and fro to greatness,
and from thence down to little more than to that
wherein she found him (a bare gentleman).

—SIR ROBERT NAUNTON

Hayes Barton as it appears today. (COURTESY JIM BATTEN)

Chapter 1

FROM DEVON TO THE WARS

Walter Ralegh was born in Devon, a sheepherding and farming county in southwest England that, to the south, borders the English Channel. His family had lived in the area since William of Normandy conquered England in 1066, and some members became judges, bishops, or knights. But by the time he was born, probably in 1554, the Raleghs were not wealthy or titled. Truth to tell, the family was in something of a decline.

Walter's father did not own the house in which he lived or the land he farmed. Hayes Barton is a two-story thatched-roof farmhouse that still stands near East Budleigh in Devon. That rented home is where Walter was born, and it looks somewhat similar today. In Hayes Wood fast-growing pine have replaced the tall stands of beech. Nearby, red cliffs face the sea. Growing up on a farm near the coast, Walter knew the wealth of the land and always felt the lure of sea.

It was easy to tell where Ralegh came from. Everyone noticed that he spoke "broad Devonshire to his dying day." Saying that a person has a Devon accent is not a compliment. It suggests he is a rube, the opposite of a London sophisticate. Ralegh's greatest rival, the Earl of Essex, called him an upstart and a knave. Yet he rose to be extremely close to Queen Elizabeth I, perhaps the greatest ruler in all of English history. The burning desire to rise from his humble origins and reach as high as ambition could take him explains a lot about Ralegh.

As a younger son, Walter did not stand to inherit anything from his father's limited estate. The one thing his father, also named Walter, could give him was introductions and connections. A gentleman farmer who was twice widowed, Walter senior used the alliances made by his three marriages to try to recover the family's fortunes. Through him Ralegh was linked to important local families, including the Drakes (think of Sir Francis) and the Gilberts. Queen Elizabeth granted Walter's half brother, Sir Humphrey Gilbert, the very first patent, or license, to create colonies in America. Adventures into the unknown, including sea battles and exploring new lands, were Walter's family heritage.

The closest thing to a Devon accent in America is the speech of the Tangierines, islanders who live off the coast of the Chesapeake Bay in Maryland. It is no coincidence that some people who live along the Atlantic Coast, from North Carolina through New Jersey, speak an English that is similar to Ralegh's. Their accents are the record of the explorations and colonies he and his neighbors planned, organized, and led.

■ ■ ■

HOW ENGLAND BECAME ENGLAND

The yearning for new lives that propelled people across the seas to explore the New World did not come merely from the ambition of a few families; it was a result of very large-scale changes that were going on throughout Europe. In the sixteenth and seventeenth centuries England become a nation.

Before the reign of Henry VIII, England was a good Catholic country. In 1521 Pope Leo X honored Henry as a Defender of the Faith for his opposition to Martin Luther and the new Protestant creed. But in a series of conflicts with Rome over his desire to divorce and remarry, the outsize and ambitious king broke away from Catholicism. By 1535 he had named himself head of the Church of England. England was no longer just another Catholic country under the spiritual rule of the pope. Now it was its own nation with its own faith.

As long as the king served the pope, and the pope served God, all of creation was securely in place. A divine order descended from God to the angels, the stars to the earth, nobles to common people, men to women, adults to children, humans to animals, animals to rocks. As William Shakespeare put it, "The heavens themselves, the planets and this centre/Observe degree, priority and place." A person's place was where he or she fit on this eternal ladder. But now, suddenly, all the links were weakening, and people began to look out to the horizon, not up to the sky.

Medieval maps centered on the Holy Land, especially Jerusalem, the City of God. The rest of the world was usually just sketched in. But Ralegh's contemporary, the playwright Christopher Marlowe, had a character say, "Give me a map; then let me see how much is left for me to conquer all the world." The old maps reaffirmed ancient truths; the new ones showed how to make new conquests. In 1579 Christopher Saxton finished compiling the very first atlas of all England. Throughout the 1590s John Norden traveled throughout the country to study the land. His long labors allowed him to create the first map of the kingdom to include roads.

When people started to look around at their country, they became increasingly interested in its history. *Gorboduc,* the first English tragedy, was performed in 1561, and it used themes from the mythological history of the island. Before then, plays retold stories of religion and faith. Now, for the first time, England itself mattered to the public. Shakespeare's many plays about the kings of England followed soon after *Gorboduc* and satisfied the public's newfound hunger to understand and celebrate the nation's past.

One reason most people's interests were confined to either local matters or heavenly revelations was that so few of them could read. Catholic law insisted that the Bible appear in Latin. One important effect of having a Protestant nation was that the Bible could now legally be translated into English.

Sir Thomas More was a thoughtful Catholic who served for a time as Henry's most important minister. His book *Utopia* was one of the first to treat the New World as a place where people might be able to create a perfect way of living. But he was against translating the Bible. He did not think it should "be in the English tongue and in the hands of common people." Instead, he wanted the holy word to remain in the control of "superiors." Henry eventually had More killed for holding so firmly to his Catholic beliefs.

Not merely were the Latin Bibles impossible to read, for almost all

English people they were also hard to find. The first books that Johannes Gutenberg printed were Bibles. Protestantism and printing fit very well together, since the new technology made it so much easier to bring Bibles to people, which is exactly what the new Protestant ministers thought should happen.

The first complete Bible in English was published in 1535–36. This sped up the radical changes that were already taking place in the English language—some ten thousand to twelve thousand new words were added between the 1400s and 1600s—and challenged how everyone from the most humble peasant to the greatest lord thought about religion. John Aubrey, a seventeenth-century writer who collected stories of earlier times, reported sadly that "printing and gunpowder have frighted away . . . the fairies." Local rituals that dated back to pre-Christian times and superstitions drawn from any number of traditions now had to compete with printed Bibles. An aggressive Protestantism supported by Bibles and guns, together with new maps and plays, was turning England into a modern nation.

While Henry began a process that tied the nation ever closer together, he also set in motion centuries of conflict. The question of what religion the government favored affected how each person in England thought, prayed, and marked the events of life. The idea of religious toleration, the belief that anyone can worship as he or she pleases, arose only as a result of precisely these struggles over religion. In sixteenth-century England, religion was not a matter of individual choice; it was a test of national loyalty.

This was especially tricky for the English, because it was not at all clear that Henry's decision to leave Catholicism and make England Protestant would survive his death. If one ruler could pull England away from Rome,

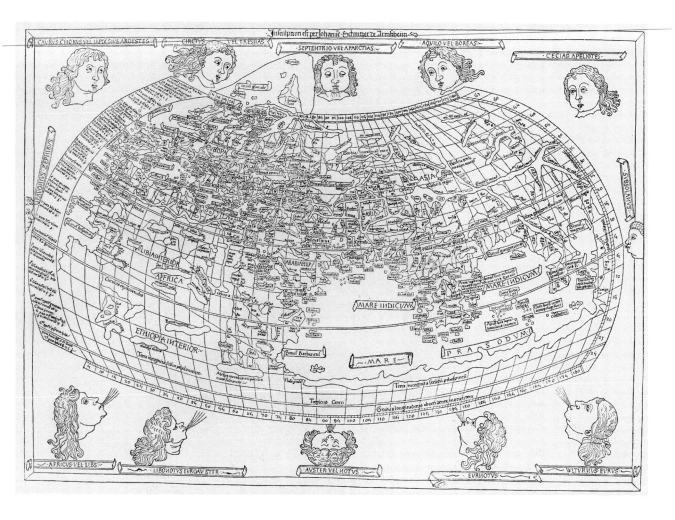

In this map from 1482 the center of the world is the Holy Land (just above ARABIA). Though other parts of the world appear in detail, none matter as much.

OPPOSITE TOP: *Devonshire, from Christopher Saxton's Atlas. Now every inch of England deserves to be mapped.* (COURTESY IAN MAXTED)

OPPOSITE BOTTOM: *In this close-up from Saxton, Ralegh's birthplace at Hayes Barton is a short way inland, near the left bank of the small river that is in the upper half of the map, midway between Sidmouth and the wider waterway that empties out at Exmouth.* (COURTESY IAN MAXTED)

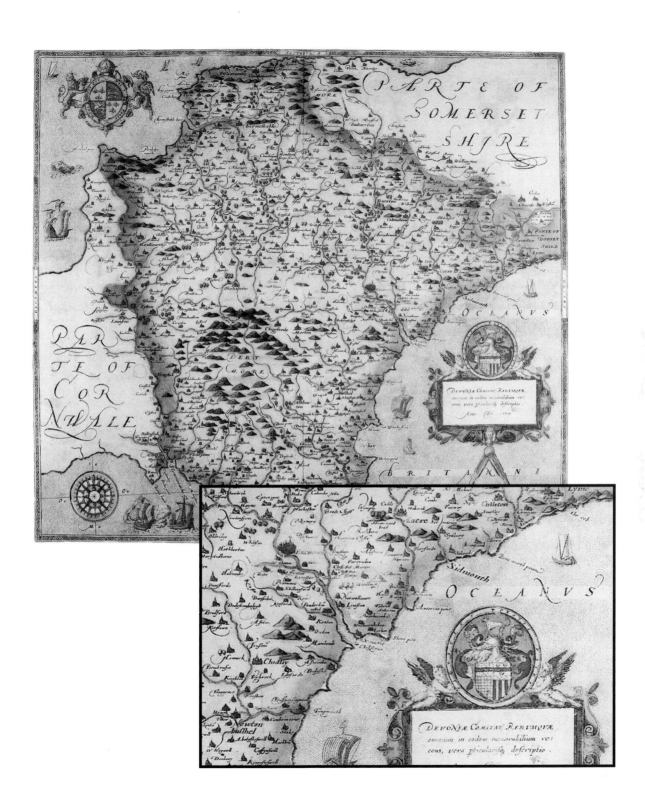

why couldn't another yank it back? The very power Henry brought to the Crown meant that the rulers who followed him could undo everything he had done.

If a new sovereign reembraced Catholicism, it would not just alter how religion was practiced in England. The twists and turns of religious policy in England had international implications. Wars over religion were ravaging Europe. The Netherlands, for example, was the site of ongoing bloody strife as Catholic Spain sought to hold on to an area it had obtained by marriage, while the Protestant northern region fought furiously for freedom. Whether England was Protestant or Catholic also determined which side it would support in these bitter conflicts. A person whose beliefs were more similar to those of an enemy nation than to those of the king or queen might very well be tempted to turn traitor, or to spy and send important secrets overseas.

What you believed could make you a loyal subject or a traitor, a heretic or a martyr, and this could change with every new ruler. A new kind of order that replaced the old ladder of faith, and endless turmoil over religion and nation—these were keynotes of Ralegh's time.

FAMILY AND FAITH

From early on, the Raleghs were Protestants. In the shifting tides of the 1500s this at first hurt and later helped them. When Walter's father spoke against a local woman for praying with her rosary beads, the pro-Catholic townspeople trapped him in a church and threatened to hang him. That religious mob was crushed by the government's army. In 1553, though, Mary I came to power. She was a Catholic who quickly imprisoned Elizabeth, her

Protestant half sister, in the Tower of London, and repealed her father's and half brother's anti-Catholic laws. Worse yet, she married the arch-Catholic King Philip II of Spain.

A cousin of Walter's mother tried to stir up a rebellion against this ominous match, and Walter senior helped him to escape when it failed. In Devon Catholic ritual was reinstated in all the churches. As well-known enemies of that faith, the Raleghs were in real danger. But in 1558 everything changed yet again. Mary died, and Elizabeth came to power. Now the Raleghs' strong stand for Protestantism not only placed them on the winning side, it allied them with the queen.

A young man driven to recover his family's fortunes, a Protestant eager to prove himself to the great Protestant queen, a son of Devon who grew up hearing tales of the lands beyond the horizon—this was Walter Ralegh as he stepped onto the stage of history.

THE MOST GRIEVOUS CALAMITY

Ralegh was always described as tall—over six feet, which was unusual in his day; strikingly handsome; and brimming with the kind of bold confidence that is between charismatic and insufferable. He made his first appearance on the historical record when he enrolled at Oriel College, Oxford, in 1568. Stories written years later tell that he was short of money and was a brilliant student. As early as 1569, though, he was in France, fighting for the Protestant cause.

French Protestants were called Huguenots, and their struggles against the Catholics were splitting the country apart. At times it seemed there was

Ralegh's mother, Catherine, came to console Agnes Prest the night before she was burned at the stake in 1557. Erected in 1909, this bas relief of Prest's death is part of the Protestant Martyrs monument in Devon.

no France, only regions controlled by one side or the other. Ralegh was related to the wife of the Comte de Montgomerie, a Huguenot leader. In joining Montgomerie's army, Ralegh was fighting for his family, his religion, his queen, and his future. No school could ever be that compelling.

When Ralegh went to France, he was a teenager, somewhere between fifteen and seventeen years old. He took part in horrific fighting. On the basis of what he experienced, Ralegh later wrote, "The greatest and most grievous calamity that can come to any state is civil war." In his first year there the Huguenots suffered an agonizing defeat at Moncontour, with over ten thousand casualties. A peace was concluded in 1570, but on August 24, 1572, Saint Bartholomew's Day, the bloodletting began again. Many important Huguenots were gathered in Paris to celebrate a royal wedding. Someone, perhaps the king's mother, ordered the assassination of the Huguenot leader. Once started, the political murders turned into mob-led massacres. The slaughter soon spread throughout Paris and to the provinces. In the end perhaps three thousand people were killed in Paris, and another ten thousand throughout France.

Not long after the massacre, when Ralegh's side trapped some Catholics in a cave, he and his men sent down bundles of lighted straw to force them out. As he later wrote, "Those that defended [the cave] were so smothered that they surrendered themselves . . . or they must have died like bees that are smoked out of their hives." Wars over human souls turned combatants into so many insects to be exterminated.

Ralegh's initial education in warfare ended in 1574, when the Comte de Montgomerie was caught and beheaded. We can only guess what effect these grim early events had on Ralegh's character. All his writings show an unusually calm and accepting attitude toward death, the one experience we are all sure to have. That understanding may well have come from being surrounded by so much suffering so early.

Seeing terrible carnage up close did not scare Ralegh at all. Rather, it made him all the more headstrong. If we are going to die anyway, he believed, why be cautious? Why not risk all now, at this moment, in this adventure? And because Ralegh showed no fear, he often won battles against tremendous odds, starting with his quest for the queen's favor.

Back in England in 1575, Ralegh registered as what we would call a lawyer in training, though the system was not much like our law school. The next year he published a poem praising a book of poetry by a soldier adventurer named George Gascoigne. Poetry may seem like an unusual interest for an ambitious young soldier or an aspiring lawyer, but in Elizabethan England it was a perfect choice. A man was valued as much for his agility with words as for his courage in battle. Ralegh excelled in both kinds of combat.

The most famous stories about Ralegh illustrate how he used his courage and his wits to charm the queen. According to Thomas Fuller:

> Ralegh . . . (his clothes being then a considerable part of his estate) found the queen walking, till, meeting with a plashy place, she seemed to scruple going thereon. Presently Ralegh cast and spread his new plush cloak on the ground; whereon the Queen trod gently over, rewarding him afterwards with many suits for his so free and seasonable tender of so fair a foot cloth.

Fuller's story fits Ralegh, the passionate daredevil who was determined to make his name known. He had little money but used what he had to purchase expensive clothing that showed off both his features and his sense of style. A taste for total risks that brought the chance of greater glory also

would have had little or no right to resist his decision. What is more, even these religious camps were split. The Spanish and Austrian Catholics were most afraid that she would marry a French Catholic, while the Lutheran and Swiss Reformed Protestants eyed each other's leading men suspiciously.

The one way Elizabeth could rule alone as a powerful monarch in England and as a feared and admired queen overseas was to make her weakness her strength. She kept considering suitors, offering them hope when she needed their aid, rejecting them when they grew insistent. She dangled her love as a prize and yet never fully granted it to any handsome noble, persuasive ambassador, or powerful king.

Elizabeth's hesitations and calculations do not imply that she was without feeling for men. She may indeed have loved Dudley, and later Essex. A courtier such as Ralegh who wooed her with charm, looks, and wit could very nearly win her. But feeling went only so far. Elizabeth could almost marry, could very seriously consider suits, could even fall in love. Yet the combination of her need to rule and the power of all of the competing factions at court meant she would never wed.

The court of love she created was half a game of chivalry and courtship and half the most cold and devious calculation of state. It was a world in which love and romance seemed to rule, and did, just as much as steely ambition and brilliant policy.

THE QUEEN'S PROGRESS

Elizabeth's flirtations took place at court, where her suitors were the greatest nobles in Europe. But she also carried out a second kind of love affair with

This engraving of Elizabeth was made in 1603 by Crispin van de Passe I based on a drawing by Isaac Oliver. Virginia, which Ralegh named for his Virgin Queen, is listed prominently in the caption as one of the territories under her rule. (BY PERMISSION OF THE FOLGER SHAKESPEARE LIBRARY)

the people of England. She did this in her speeches and in her lavish travels around the country.

Every summer Elizabeth would go on a progress. She and the huge retinue of ladies-in-waiting, courtiers, advisers, soldiers, visitors, and officials who surrounded her could remain in one place only so long. Soon even the largest castle would be so filthy, malodorous, and disease-ridden that the royal party had to move on. For Elizabeth this necessity became an opportunity. Each progress gave her a chance to visit another part of the realm and to bond with her subjects. Even the Spanish ambassador noticed that "she was received everywhere with great acclamations and signs of joy." In turn, each wealthy lord who had the honor of housing the queen was expected to give her lavish gifts. Every visit was a test of the loyalty of nobles and regions, and a celebration of the great queen whose love united England.

In the spring of 1578, around the time Ralegh came to the court, Elizabeth was afflicted with a problem no one had the courage to solve. She suffered from a terrible toothache, and the sole remedy would be to have it removed, a painful operation. Not even William Cecil, Lord Burghley, her Lord Treasurer and most important minister, would risk telling her she would have to endure an extraction. In the end, she never got the bad news, and she was in pain all summer.

This story holds several keys to understanding Elizabeth and her time. Though she was a rational, coolly calculating ruler who outthought her more powerful rivals around the globe, she was also temperamental and emotional. Her mood mattered. If she got angry enough, no one was safe. The things that could upset her were often associated with love: Who was the fairest queen? Did love for her overrule all other passions? Elizabeth had to be courted as a lover even as she had to be honored as a queen. And in both pursuits one had to be dead serious. Inconstancy and disloyalty were the worst crimes of all.

On the other hand, Elizabeth's favorites—the men who helped her run the country—were treated as something between pets and lovers. They all had nicknames: The Earl of Leicester was called Eyes; Lord Burghley, her Spirit; Francis Walsingham, her all-seeing spymaster, who could be quite critical, an Ethiopian for his dark moods; Ralegh, in a soft dig at his thick accent, Water. Christopher Hatton, a most loyal favorite, was known as Lids, or her Bellwether.

When Hatton saw that Ralegh had caught Elizabeth's eye, he sent the queen some gifts, including a small water bucket. She sent him back a dove and reminded him that in the story of Noah and the flood the bird, "together with the rainbow, brought the covenant that there should be no more destruction by water." Water (Walter) would never rise too high, her gift reassured Hatton—but only as part of the game in which Elizabeth played the part of the Old Testament god.

Toothache or no, on July 11 Elizabeth set out on her progress, surrounded by gentleman pensioners with gold chains and ceremonial spearhead-topped battle-axes. By July 27 the royal party reached Cambridge. After various learned men spoke in Latin and presented gifts of Bibles and gloves, everyone retired to the home of the Earl of Leicester. There they held a mock debate on which were the best qualities required for a just ruler. Elizabeth was an accomplished linguist and had read widely in the classics. When she was sixteen, her childhood tutor, the scholar Roger Ascham, wrote that she "talks French and Italian as well as she does in English, and has often talked to me readily and well in Latin, moderately in Greek. When she writes Greek and Latin, nothing is more beautiful than her handwriting." She later learned some Spanish. Scholarship and word games that relied on knowing references in many languages always appealed to the queen.

In mid-June officers of Norwich, then the second-largest city in England, were warned that the queen would arrive in mid-August. Though much smaller than London, Norwich was an important textile center. Teams scurried to clean up the city. They had to improve the roadway into town as well as the main street. Citizens were told that they had to clean and plaster the sides of their homes that faced the street. And anyone who did not have a convenient privy had to make new arrangements, for, during her visit, the townspeople would not be allowed to follow their usual custom of spilling waste onto the streets.

Queen Elizabeth reached Norwich on August 16. As she approached, the city officers, accompanied by sixty of the most "comely young men," rode to meet her. These handsome riders wore special clothing: "black satin doublets, black hose, black taffeta hats with yellow bands, and purple taffeta mandelions (long jackets with hanging sleeves and open seams) decorated with silver lace." When the parties met, the crowd went wild. A contemporary chronicle reported that "hardly for a great time could anything be heard."

The queen's passage around the city was like a cross between a ride in a modern theme park and a school pageant. She arrived at displays and events that retold local legends or history, and that bonded city and sovereign. Outside the city walls she met a man wearing a black velvet hat with white feathers who was dressed in armor over green and white silk. He represented King Gurgant, a mythological character who was said to have built a castle in Norwich. As she passed through St. Stephen's Gate into the city itself, five musicians played. These waits, as they were called, were employed by the city to honor special occasions and were particularly renowned. They all wore silver chains, and their instruments had small flags attached to them.

The queen rested on Sunday and remained indoors because of bad weather on Monday. But the locals were not deterred. They had prepared to show "what pastime the Gods had provided for a noble Prince." That evening a strange contraption drew up to her castle window. A coach was covered with cutout images of birds, sprites, and clouds that quivered as it moved. It also sported a lavishly painted and bejeweled tower topped with spangled white feathers. This ancestor of all parade floats was drawn by painted horses with costume wings and carried a trumpeter to herald the god Mercury himself. Clad in blue satin lined with gold, Mercury had wings on his hat and heels, as well as on his traditional golden rod with its two wriggling serpents.

The coachmen had orders to drive the horses so fast they would "seem to fly." As the cantering hoofs clattered to a halt, the trumpeter sounded a call, and Mercury jumped down to bring his message from the gods to the queen. His mission was to

> *Tell her that she is to me so dear*
> *That I appoint by man's device and art*
> *That every day she shall see sundry shows*
> *If that she please to walk and take the air;*
> *And that so soon as out of doors she goes*
> *(If time do serve and weather waxeth fair)*
> *Some odd device shall meet her Highness straight*
> *To make her smile and ease her burdened breast.*

As Elizabeth left for a deer hunt the next day, she met Cupid and Venus and was treated to an allegory in which Chastity, Modesty, and Temperance contested with Wantonness and Riot. For a Virgin Queen a celebration of chastity seemed just the thing, and one song said that:

> Chaste life lives long and looks on world and wicked ways;
> Chaste life for loss of pleasures short doth win immortal praise
> Lewd life cuts off his days and soon runs out his date
> Confounds good wits, breeds naughty blood and weakens man's estate.

The linking of hunting and chastity was no accident, for it called to mind Diana, a Roman goddess closely associated with Elizabeth. Diana was a huntress yet the goddess of animals, a virgin yet the fierce protector of women in childbirth. The pure white light of the moon was hers as well. In Elizabeth's day huge tracts of land were reserved as royal deer parks. That is why there are so many folktales about poaching and the consequences of killing royal stags.

A royal hunt was as well planned as a progress. Beaters would drive animals into an enclosure, where Elizabeth would kill them with her crossbow or watch while dogs tore them apart. The hunt celebrated rule, power, authority. Elizabeth was an enthusiastic huntress. Like Diana she was a virgin warrior. Throughout her reign, people courted her by praising virginity in their plays, poems, and prose.

The following day an elaborate show, planned for barges on a river the queen would pass, had to be canceled when darkness arrived before she did. Still, she did hear a local grammar school teacher address her in Latin. He was terrified, but she told him to "be not afraid." At the end she remarked

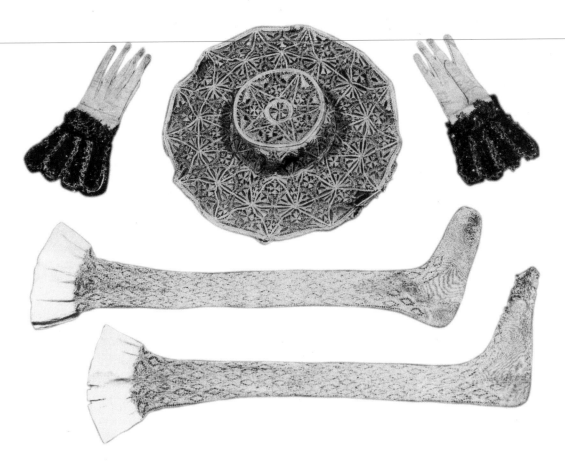

Elizabeth is thought to have left these gloves behind on her way to Norwich. The hat and stockings may well have been hers, too.

that his talk was "the best that I ever heard." While Elizabeth could be fearsome to her closest counselors, she won the love of her subjects by treating them as people who mattered to her.

Friday brought Elizabeth's visit to Norwich to a close. As she rode through the streets, she saw homes garlanded with flowers, pictures, and banners.

Amidst all the fun and good feeling the progress accomplished some serious state business. Throughout the visit, the queen's ministers searched out secret Catholics. Being in a region they seldom visited gave them a chance to check up on people whose loyalty was in question. Doubtless the presence of a lavish and beloved royal party also impressed on any who had rebellious ideas what they were up against.

For people who had never seen their great ruler and surely would never see her again, these were events to remember for a lifetime. They reminded everyone from the poorest farmer to the wealthiest noble of the beliefs that held England together.

In great halls and on makeshift city stages, in lavish displays and bloody hunts, in skits by amateur scribblers and plays by Shakespeare came the same message: Elizabeth was the great Virgin Queen, the incarnation of Diana the huntress. She was human enough to praise stuttering Latin, and grand enough to please the gods. Under her care, her kingdom would surely prosper.

As Walter Ralegh responded to the challenge his queen set out on the windowpane, he had to master the language of love and theater that ruled her court. But to take a real part in that grand game he had to overcome the obstacles of his birth. He was poor, not of noble family; and he had to make his way without allies or sponsors. In order for Ralegh to begin wooing Elizabeth, he needed to establish his reputation and earn his fortune. The only way for him to begin his "climb" at court was to leave England and take to the sea.

Chapter 3

PLANTATIONS

When Ralegh left England, he took everything admirable and repugnant within English society with him. An outsider trying to rise, he sympathized with outsiders, but he joined in the brutal oppression of the Irish. He felt all his desires so strongly they were like "scalding fire." That driving ambition was precisely the quality needed to risk the high seas, no matter what the cost, or consequence.

England came to the grand game of overseas ambition late. By the time Ralegh was born, the Spanish had already conquered the three wealthy New World kingdoms. The Portuguese had sailed around Africa and established a rich trade in gold and ivory (and soon slaves) with west African kings. Late arrivals with low budgets, the English were limited to piracy or finding new lands.

In 1578, the year of the Norwich progress, Sir Humphrey Gilbert received his patent from Elizabeth to "discover, search, find out and view such remote heathen and barbarous lands . . . not actually possessed of any Christian prince or people." Though English sailors had been exploring in the New World for some time, Gilbert was the first to set out with the aim of creating an English colony. Inspired, perhaps, by More's vision of Utopia, Gilbert wanted to create an extension of England overseas. Ralegh was eager to join in the adventure with his half brother.

One English version of the quest for El Dorado was the search for a new trade route that would avoid the Spanish and yet lead to the wealth of Asia. Martin Frobisher's explorations in what is now Baffin Bay, Canada, had just shown that this cold territory did not hold much promise. Yet Gilbert still hoped to find a warmer site for English settlers on the northern waters. Ten well-armed ships and 365 men sailed from Plymouth on September 26, 1578, but bad weather soon returned them to port. The single ship to reach the sea was the *Falcon*, captained by Walter Ralegh. The ship's navigator was a Portuguese pilot named Simon Fernandez. Ralegh's only reward for the combination of obstinacy and courage he displayed in plunging ahead through the storms was to be roundly beaten by the Spanish ships he ran into off the Azores.

Neither Ralegh nor Gilbert was discouraged, for they had another option. Even before he ever considered America, Gilbert had his eye on Ireland. In Ireland lay a very different kind of overseas adventure: Ireland was the site of English plantations.

Americans usually think of a plantation as a large farm in the prewar American South, with gangs of slaves working cotton and a white-columned mansion in the background. But the word can mean either any area under cultivation or a settlement in a new land. That second sense is exactly the same as a colony. That is why the first Pilgrim settlement was called Plymouth Plantation.

For Gilbert and for Ralegh there was a kind of hopeful optimism in establishing plantations. If successful, the sponsors—men like them— would rise to take their place among the wealthiest in the land. And away from long-standing duties and prejudices, even the humble people who worked the soil could better themselves.

From the days of Mary on, the English tried to establish plantations in Ireland. Here the darker side of English colonial ambitions showed itself, and it was just as real as More's, Gilbert's, or Ralegh's grand dreams and high ideals. The plan was to drive Catholic, Gaelic-speaking Irish people off their land. Then English settlers could be planted on this new soil, bringing with them Protestantism, order, and links with their homeland. The brilliant and cold Francis Bacon, Ralegh's contemporary, described the Irish as "the last daughters of Europe" to be "reclaimed from . . . savage and barbarous customs to humanity and civility."

Ireland was the model for an English colony. Just across the Irish Sea the English experimented with creating real communities of farmers and sol- diers. In particular, Ireland was a training ground for the men who would later sail across the Atlantic. But what were the English learning in their model colonies?

Some historians believe that the worst English prejudice against the native peoples of America was formed in their struggles with the Irish. The Irish used the kind of terrifying ambush tactics the English would encounter in America. In Ireland in just this period Edmund Spenser wrote *The Faerie Queene*, one of the most famous poems in English history. He described the Irish as "vile caitive [despicable] wretches, ragged, rude, deformed."

The English brought this nightmare image of savagery with them to America. As they began to fight against native peoples in the New World, they treated them just as they had the Irish. Some astute observers saw how misguided and dangerous this was. In 1637 Roger Williams, the founder of Rhode Island, warned the Puritans that if they did not treat the Indians well, they would "turn wild Irish."

"Irish" had become a byword for fierce and barbaric, for those who resist civilization and order. While plantations were meant to give the English a new chance to rise, and even to offer better government and religion to the Catholic Irish, they could be built only by treating Catholicism as vile and the Irish as subhuman. Unfortunately, Ralegh was one of those callous Englishmen. There is good evidence that he helped direct a massacre in Ireland. Acting as the agent of a group that thought of itself as the force of order, he behaved savagely.

By August of 1580 Ralegh was in Ireland, fighting alongside a number of Devonshire relations to protect and expand English interests. Within weeks one cousin was killed in an ambush and another had a narrow escape. In retrospect, Ralegh wrote that "certainly the miseries of war are never so bitter and many as when a whole nation . . . forsaking their own seats, labor to root out the established possession of another land, making room for themselves, their wives and children. . . . The merciless terms of this controversy arm both sides with desperate resolution." His chance to show how "merciless" came within months.

Recruited by the pope, who armed them with his decree excommunicating Elizabeth, and largely sponsored by Philip II of Spain, a contingent of six hundred to eight hundred Italian, Spanish, and Basque mercenaries sailed to Ireland. After a short time an unknown number left. Under the leadership

Drawn in the 1570s by John Derrick, an Englishman, just when Ralegh was fighting in Ireland, this woodcut shows his belief that the powerful and orderly English were crushing the savage, long-haired Irish.

(FROM DERRICK'S *THE IMAGE OF IRELAND*)

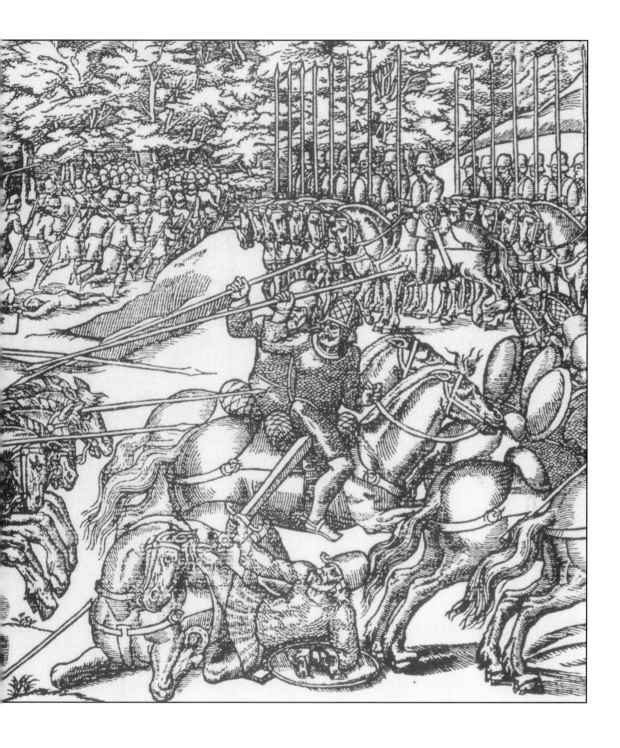

of a rebellious nobleman named James Fitzmaurice, as many as two hundred Irish men and women may have joined with their fellow Catholics in Smerwick on the western coast of the island. Had the mercenaries and Irish held their ground and inspired further pro-Catholic rebellions throughout the island, they could have posed a serious threat to the Crown. Ireland in flames would have preoccupied the English and perhaps even set off religious and civil war at home. While Ireland offered England fertile soil to plant colonies, it gave the country's enemies equally receptive ground to sow rebellion.

English forces under Lord Grey soon laid siege to the Smerwick fort, and on November 9 (or 10 or 11) the enemy surrendered. There is some controversy over the terms under which the Catholics gave themselves up. Did they lay down their arms from a position of strength because they thought they were going to be spared? Or were they fighting a lost battle from a crumbling fort, in which case unconditional surrender was the only option? In other words, did Lord Grey make a treacherous offer of mercy because he had no other way to win? Or did he offer nothing at all, because he didn't need to?

Whatever Grey did or did not agree to, once the Irish set down their arms, he ordered Ralegh and a fellow officer to lead their men into the fort, take a very few valuable prisoners, and kill everyone else. They did.

At times Ralegh had an idealistic bent, and he acted with concern for the sufferings of others even at some risk to himself. But he could act with cold determination. He did what he had to do. That made him a brave and formidable soldier. When faced with his own death, he was stoic and eloquent. As he did not fear death, he did not hesitate before it. And he could kill without compunction.

Ralegh was a complex man who was as comfortable writing passionate poems as he was fighting gruesome battles. He spoke for religious toleration, and yet he could treat Catholic enemies as bees to be smoked out. He prided himself on being more compassionate to the native peoples of America than were the Spanish, and proved that in action. And yet he led a massacre in Ireland. Somewhere in that cross-section of grim ambition, battle-born will, and yearning for a better life is a key not only to Ralegh but to his age. For it was just this spirit that led directly to the colonization of British North America. If the settlers of Jamestown were the heirs of his striving for a better life, so too were they the children of his cold purpose.

GALLANT CAPTAIN

Most of the fighting in Ireland was quite different from the large siege at Smerwick. Guerrilla war with its quick and deadly clashes perfectly suited Ralegh's temperament. Here his bravery was heroic and his coolness under fire terrifying to his enemies. In the winter of 1581, for example, he and six men were surprised between two rivers by sixty soldiers accompanied by fifteen horsemen. Ralegh fought his way through the enemy ranks. When he saw that a fellow Devonshireman was left behind, he turned back to save him. Armed only with a pistol, a staff, and his unflinching courage, he faced down the enemy until all his men were safe.

A soldier with Ralegh's zeal who wins battles against great odds soon draws attention. By the spring of 1582 he was given a temporary appointment as one of three men to run the county of Munster, which then occupied about a quarter of Ireland. The younger son of a farmer from Devon was now in command of a huge tract of land. That spurred him to take greater risks.

Ralegh set off with a small group of horsemen to capture a nobleman named Lord Roche, who was said to be a traitor. The very Irish leader whom Ralegh had fought off between the rivers waited in ambush with eight hundred men. Forewarned, Ralegh evaded their trap by marching all night. Arriving at Roche's castle at dawn, he entered with just five men. But he told the rest of his crew to filter into the castle casually and to occupy all its key positions. With a tiny force Ralegh arrested the lord in his own keep and marched him back under cover of night when none of his supporters were awake.

As soon as Ralegh scored these impressive victories, he made sure the court heard about them. After all, Ireland was just a way station to his larger aims. The eager soldier dashed off letters describing his daring capture of the lord to two of the queen's most important counselors, Walsingham and the Earl of Leicester. He asked for a castle as a reward, and somewhere along the way he was made captain. But having gained what he could from adventures in Ireland, he was really most eager to return home. There he would find out just how much of a name he had made.

Chapter 4

FORTUNE'S FAVOR

The portrait of Ralegh on the following page, dated 1588, shows us how perfectly he played the game of courtly love. He faces us, but his head is slightly turned so that his pearl earring is clearly displayed. The pearl was a symbol of virginity. Ralegh's lavish jacket shows his wealth, as does his pearl-drenched cape. Rumor had it that he wore hundreds of thousands of pounds' worth of jewels in his clothing. His hand is delicately outspread across a tabletop. Elizabeth was vain about her hands and took every chance to show them. His gesture echoes hers while also displaying his own attractive features.

Moving straight up the canvas from the hand, the viewer's eye comes to Ralegh's motto, *amor et virtute,* followed by a sliver of Diana's moon. All of Ralegh's silver-and-black clothing is suggestive of wealth and symbolic of virginity and yet sets him off as a dashing, perhaps dangerous, man.

Ralegh in 1588. (Courtesy the National Portrait Gallery, London)

Once back in England, Ralegh shifted away from his role as a brave captain and courted his queen in his appearance, with gifts, and especially in wit and words. Their most famous conversation was about tobacco. One day he bet Elizabeth that he could weigh the very smoke a tobacco pipe produced. Puzzled yet willing, she agreed. Ralegh took out some tobacco and carefully placed it on a scale. He then put it into his pipe and enjoyed a leisurely smoke. Then he weighed the ashes. The difference between the two, he stated triumphantly, could only be the smoke. Elizabeth paid up, adding her own sharp turn of phrase. She allowed that she knew of people "who turned gold into smoke, but Ralegh was the first who turned smoke into gold."

Much of Ralegh's poetry was similar to this exchange of wit. He wrote it to give to his queen as a gift, a sign of his cleverness, learning, and devotion. Toward the end of the 1580s Ralegh wrote a poem about Diana:

> *Praised be Diana's fair and harmless light,*
> *Praised be the dews, wherewith she moists the ground;*
> *Praised be her beams, the glory of the night,*
> *Praised be her power, by which all powers abound. . . .*
>
> *Time wears her not, she doth his chariot guide,*
> *Mortality below her orbe is placed;*
> *By her the virtue of the stars down slide;*
> *In her is virtue's perfect image cast.*
>   *A knowledge pure it is her worth to know,*
>   *With Circes let them dwell that think not so.*

Ralegh's poem celebrates the queen in ways that are reminiscent of the

Norwich progress. Elizabeth is Diana, goddess of forest dew, of the moon, the center of power for her nation. Yet there are some personal notes that show how his mind worked. When this poem was written, Elizabeth was in her fifties. Saying that she is immune to time and change is a clever gambit. Ralegh the courtier flattered a vain, aging queen by declaring her immune to change. But he also needed her to be that. She resides beyond the sun. The mortal world of change and decay exists only beneath her orbit. She is literally above it.

In this poem Queen Elizabeth holds all of creation together in calm, perfect order. That must have been exactly what Ralegh felt. For she was the sun, the star, the center of his universe. She could grant him any favor and keep his enemies at bay—so long as she accepted his worship as pure.

Charmed by Ralegh the man, admiring of Ralegh the bold soldier, intrigued by Ralegh the clever poet, Elizabeth showered him with royal favor. In 1583 she gave him access to a palatial home in London, then granted him control of two estates to help pay the rent. From a turret in Durham House he could now look out over the Thames River. John Aubrey wrote that the view was as "pleasant, perhaps, as any in the world, and which not only refreshes the eyesight but cheers the spirits, and (to my mind) I believe enlarges an ingenious man's thoughts." Ralegh's spirits certainly were cheered by Elizabth's gifts, which only enlarged his ambitions.

While there were charges in Elizabeth's England similar to our tariffs and taxes, they worked very differently from the fees we pay today. Elizabeth permitted only certain people to conduct key businesses, and she allowed her favorites to collect taxes for their own benefit. Fees and licenses were royal favors, not laws that applied equally to all. That May she gave Ralegh the patent, or charge, on those who sold wine. The following year he got a license to export woolen broadcloth, one of England's most valuable goods. These grants brought him an annual income that was the rough equivalent of a million dollars today.

Like many people who work their way up, Ralegh was a careful manager. People quickly came to resent this arrogant upstart who was wringing the last coin out of unpopular taxes. It was one thing to owe an ancient tribute to an inattentive yet grand noble; it was another to have a sharp-eyed newcomer collect every time a merchant tried to sell some cloth. In 1584 Elizabeth removed a tiny bit of that sting by knighting Ralegh. But a knight had only the slightest toehold on noble status, and Sir Walter had no intention of remaining on the lowest rung.

Walter Ralegh was a young man on the rise. This carried as many dangers as it did rewards. If Elizabeth was always looking for fresh talent, there were many who detested those who stepped out of their place. In that early poetic praise of Gascoigne's book, Ralegh wrote:

> *For who so reaps renown above the rest,*
> *With heaps of hate, shall surely be oppressed.*

Most people thought the brash outsider who had dazzled the queen and didn't care who knew it was "damnable proud." But Ralegh defied them: "If any man accuseth me to my face, I will answer him with my mouth; but my tail is good enough to return an answer to such who traduceth [slanders] me behind my back." And he was revered in Devon. Still another honor that came from the queen gave him a unique opportunity to do well by his countrymen. She made him Lord Warden of the Stannaries—that is, responsible for governing tin-mining privileges in Devon and its neighbor Cornwall, two counties where mining tin was an important yet hazardous and low-paying industry. In return for his interest, the people of Devon stood by him. The year he became a knight, he was also elected as one of Devon's two representatives in Parliament. In Devon he was seen as the local hero who still remembered where he came from.

With new wealth, the queen's favor, and loyal support at home, Ralegh was ready to play for really big stakes. He had risen from a farmhouse to a grand London home. From there the next step was to become one of the lords of the land. To accomplish that, he would need more than England could offer. Once again, to ensure his fortune at home, he needed a triumph across the seas.

The Lost Colony

To seek new worlds, for gold, for praise, for glory.

—Sir Walter Ralegh

Chapter 5

NEAR TO HEAVEN BY SEA

W e can imagine it this way: a small group of scholars at Durham House along with pilots and sailors, perhaps a wizard with his black cap and white beard, and, at the center, the dashing Ralegh in his black and pearls. Great maps are spread across wooden tables beside diaries, logs, and reports in many languages. As the men peer into the blank spaces at the edges of the parchments, they slowly add lines. Coasts begin to take shape. America is emerging out of legend into fact. Ralegh leads the way. He pushes forward into the blank spaces, bringing his own lore and legends with him.

As we have seen, Ralegh's first guide and inspiration in setting out onto the treacherous seas was his half brother, Sir Humphrey Gilbert. Gilbert held the patent to find new lands across the Atlantic. By 1583 Ralegh was able to give serious support to the cause. That year he contributed the equivalent of more than half a million dollars, as well as a well-armed speedy boat named the *Bark Ralegh,* to a new expedition headed by Gilbert. By the terms of Gilbert's plan, if the group took possession of good land, Ralegh would earn a 400,000-acre plot. This was the most direct way for him to become a great lord.

Elizabeth had lost money on Gilbert's ill-fated expedition in 1578 and was dubious about this one. She would not even let Gilbert lead it, saying he was "a man of no good hap by sea." Whether she meant he was unlucky or a bad captain is not clear. Using his best powers of persuasion, Ralegh convinced his queen to relent and send Gilbert out to sea. This determined both men's fates, for Gilbert was once again unlucky.

Aside from claiming Newfoundland for England, Gilbert accomplished little. After a series of wrecks and frustrations his tiny, battered fleet set sail for home. To show confidence and solidarity with his men, he remained in a small, frail boat instead of shifting to a more stable craft. Though his ship was tossed by "terrible seas," he sat calmly and read. In all likelihood the book was More's *Utopia,* the inspiration for his voyages. As the *Golden Hind* passed him, he called out, "We are as near to heaven by sea as by land." Quite near, for he and his ship soon vanished without a trace.

The year after Gilbert disappeared, Ralegh was granted a new version of his half brother's patent to "discover . . . remote . . . lands . . . not actually possessed of any Christian prince." Ralegh was now the most powerful and committed advocate of the New World in all England.

Sir Walter was assisted in his great venture by a small group of farseeing and dedicated men. They pieced together maps, legends, rumors, secret intelligence reports, and even occult soundings of the beyond to figure what lay across the seas. Among them were two cousins, both named Richard

Hakluyt. The younger one remembered how he had been fired with the dream of exploration. When still a boy, he visited his cousin and found

> Certain books of Cosmography, with a universal Map; he seeing me somewhat curious . . . pointed with his wand to all the known Seas, Gulfs, Bays, Straights, Capes, Rivers, Empires, Kingdoms, Dukedoms and Territories of each part. . . . From the Map he brought me to the Bible and turning to the 107th Psalm, directed me to the 23rd and 24th verses, where I read that "they which go down to the sea in ships and occupy great waters, these see the work of the lord, and his wonders in the deep."

To the Hakluyts a world atlas was a cross between a book of fairy tales and a holy script. It contained mysteries for the inquiring mind and magnificent quests for the stalwart explorer. Knowledge was precious, and even locating faraway lands brought a sense of wonder. The Hakluyts were as pragmatic as the most precise mapmaker and as open to the unknown as a wand-wielding magus. Just as Elizabeth could be both Diana and the head of her nation's Christian church, the rational men who peered across the seas were quite willing to believe in marvels.

One of the most interesting men of this fascinating period was the Welsh astrologer, alchemist, mathematician, and mapmaker John Dee. With his black skullcap and long white beard Dee looked exactly like what he was thought to be: a wizard. Dee was an early ally of the older Hakluyt and had drawn up an important map of the coastline of northern America in 1580. In exchange for his services Gilbert offered him any land that lay above 50 degrees north latitude (essentially all of Canada).

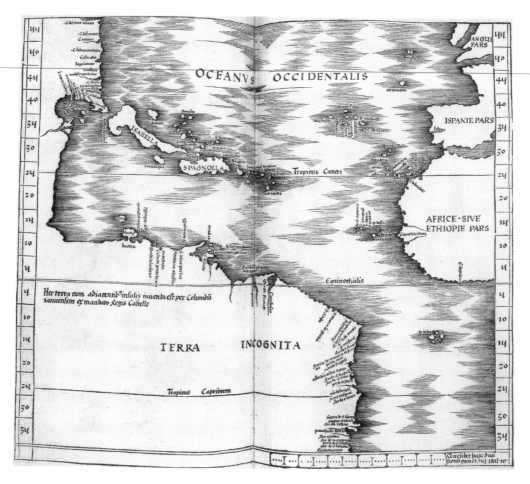

Filling in the map: the New World as Europeans saw it in 1513 and then in 1540. This map shows almost all of South America as "terra incognita," an unknown land. Only a few islands and the bare outline of the coast have been marked.

Dee carefully recorded what was known of the coastline, and his map made it seem as if a passage through northern waters from the Atlantic to the Pacific would not be hard to find. He also held séances to enlist the aid of spirits in finding those crucial pathways to the East. Dee may have seen the passage as something more than a physical place or an economic resource.

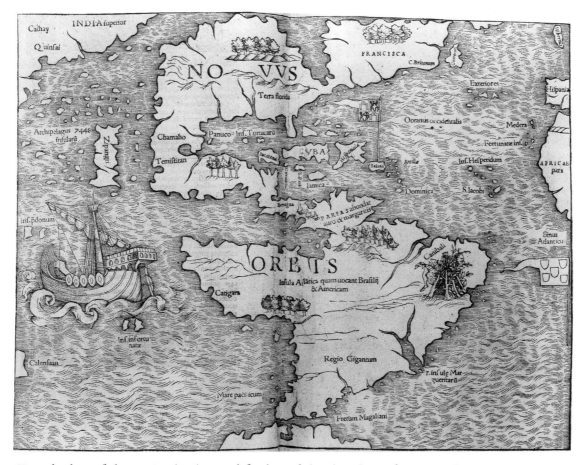

Here, the shape of the two Americas is more defined. Just below the Isthmus of Panama, the map reads "Parias abunder auro": Paria (the region inland from the coast opposite Trinidad) is abundant in gold. This is just where Ralegh went to look for it.

Like a hidden opening in an ancient myth, it could be found only by the pure of spirit.

Dee's occult interests did not make him any less devoted to reason. He advised Ralegh that his biggest need was a topnotch mathematician. Only someone both careful and ingenious with numbers could plot maps and work out navigation. A math genius who could help navigate through so many uncharted, or half-charted, seas would be invaluable.

Thomas Hariot, whom Ralegh found at Oxford, was the perfect man for the job. From 1583 straight through to 1595 he gave private lectures to Ralegh's men that made them some of the best-informed pilots and captains in Europe. Observant and curious, Hariot would play an important role in Ralegh's first great American adventure.

Dee's maps did more than define territory; they sold people on the exciting prospects across the seas. As they gathered information about the New World, advocates of exploration had to be propagandists as well as scientists. A rich merchant named William Sanderson was convinced and became the chief backer for Ralegh's efforts across the Atlantic.

Working with the Hakluyts, Dee, Hariot, and Sanderson, Ralegh possessed the money, the knowledge, and the royal connections to stake English claims in America. But he himself could not make the trip. The queen showered gifts on the dark, elegant courtier because of her fondness for him. For that very reason she would never let him out of her sight. Ralegh remained near money and power, while his men sailed off the edges of the map.

Chapter 6

A LAND OF PLENTY

On April 27, 1584, ships captained by Philip Amadas and Arthur Barlowe set sail from England. Ralegh's men knew enough not to go to the far north, where there were few resources and it was very cold. But they also could not head too far to the south, where they would surely run into the Spanish. They needed a landfall that was somewhere in the middle—warm enough to be easily habitable, yet far enough up the coast to be safe. Once people were planted in such a spot, Ralegh's patent would be in force. He would control the land that stretches north-south over much of modern North Carolina and Virginia, and west to Drake's landfall in what is now San Francisco Bay. Since no one had any idea of the size of the continent, there was no way to know what a gigantic claim this was.

A central location along the Atlantic coast had one more immediate and practical use. A deep and protected harbor would provide a great launching site for raids on the Spanish. In Ralegh's day most people set sail to the New World for some profitable piracy that could aid in the struggle against Spain. This was reinforced by the very path ships had to take to America. They followed familiar routes to the Canary Islands and then across to the Caribbean before skirting Spanish Florida and finally heading up the unknown coast. At every stage a boat bound for new shores stood a good chance of making money by capturing fishing boats, merchant vessels, even Spanish treasure ships.

Amadas and Barlowe followed exactly this route and reached the West Indies by June 10. Their pilot was Simon Fernandez, whom we first met when Ralegh set out in the *Falcon* in 1578. Fernandez had been exploring these waters for some time, and he claimed to know them well. True to his word, he conducted the crew to what is now known as the Outer Banks of North Carolina. They made landfall at a sandy island that the natives called Hatarask and the English named Port Ferdinando in his honor. On July 13 they formally claimed the land for England.

Barlowe left an account of what they saw:

> We viewed the land about us, being, whereas we first landed, very sandy and low towards the water's side, but so full of grapes as the very beating and surge of the sea overflowed them, of which we found such plenty, as well there as in all places else, both on the sand on the green soil of the hills, as in the plains, as well on every little shrub, as also climbing towards the tops of high cedars, that I think in the world the like abundance is not to be found.

This was one image of America: the infinitely fruitful, fertile land. The new land seemed to be so rich, and so nearly untouched, that hope was boundless.

The first contacts with native peoples only confirmed that image. Barlowe's report was essentially advertising copy, tailored to sound as good as possible, yet it is revealing. He wrote: "We were entertained with all love and kindness and with as much bounty, after their manner, as they could possibly devise. We found the people the most gentle loving and faithful, void of all guile and treason, and such as lived after the manner of the Golden Age." On the shores of a new land, the Greek myth of a golden age and the possibility of a golden land blended together. According to Barlowe, America was an El Dorado because it was a kind of Eden.

The brother of a local chief traded goods with the English and introduced them to what Barlowe called "their country corn, which is very white, fair and well tasted." Corn means grain in England, so this was his first taste of what the English generally call maize and we (to add to the confusion) name sweet corn. When the English visited a tiny village on the nearby island of Roanoke, they found "nine houses, built of cedar, and fortified round about with sharp trees, to keep out their enemies." Barlowe was amazed at how they were treated, "a more kind and loving people there can not be found in the world." To complete this happy picture, two young men agreed to come with the English: Manteo, who was related to an important chief, and Wanchese.

When Ralegh's men returned to England with their two exotic guests, they spread the most enthusiastic reports about what they had found. Hariot taught Manteo and Wanchese enough English for them to make a good impression and in turn learned some Algonquian from them. The explorers admitted that they had not found a good harbor. But the story of America the bountiful now seemed to be confirmed, and Ralegh supplied just the right touch when he changed the name of the land from the natives' Ossomocomuck to Virginia in honor of his queen. From his point of view the land was virgin territory, which made it the perfect place to dedicate to the Virgin Queen.

In reality the land was not virgin at all. Instead, it was a carefully managed resource. The soil of the Outer Banks is thin and sandy. Trees and vines prosper, creating an image of abundance, but this is not lush land. The natives had already found and were cultivating the best spots. They knew how to manage two plantings of corn and how to rotate these crops with squash. There were plenty of fish, but the natives had developed special reed traps that the English never mastered. While to most English the natives seemed flush with overabundant natural resources, they were actually just successful at using what they had. How they lived was perfectly suited to where they lived. This also meant they had only so much extra to spare.

Another flaw in Ralegh's plan to establish a claim in America was exposed by the makeup of a second expedition he organized the following year. The five hundred to one thousand people who left for Virginia in April of 1585 were sent as employees of the promoters who paid for the trip. Some were probably well-off adventurers who would share in whatever earnings came from the expedition. Most were either specialists, such as the German Jewish metallurgist Joachim Ganz, who were checking out new terrain for their sponsors, or soldiers doing difficult duty for a good wage. These were not individuals choosing to cross the seas to establish new farms and new lives, which is one reason there were no women. Rather, Ralegh hired available men so that his investors could see a profit. If the land proved not to be so fertile, or the natives not so friendly, men working for wages would have little incentive to stick around, especially when there was easy money to be made on the high seas.

Seven boats sailed from Plymouth harbor in Devon on April 9, 1585. The fleet was under the command of Ralegh's cousin Sir Richard Grenville in the *Tiger,* a ship lent by the queen. The boat itself has a place in literature, for Shakespeare mentions it in the first act of *Macbeth.* There a witch warns that the husband of a woman who slighted her was sent away "to Aleppo gone, master o' the *Tiger.*"

Scattered on the other boats were four men who, with Grenville, determined the fate of the settlement. There was the familiar pilot Simon Fernandez; Ralph Lane, a soldier who became governor of the colony; Thomas Hariot; and an artist named John White, who had first sailed across the Atlantic and sketched the people he saw in 1578. If you group Grenville with Fernandez (though they did not like each other at all), set Lane by himself, and link Hariot and White, you have a portrait of what America meant to England. Though the first two were eager to go to sea, they always saw the main action in taking prizes from the Spanish. Lane viewed the trip as a military challenge. Hariot and White were fascinated with the new land and new people.

As so often happened in these early days, weather, miscalculation, and mishaps took their toll. Grenville lingered for too long in the Caribbean, playing pirate. When Fernandez tried to bring the *Tiger* to the island of Ocracoke, it ran aground and invaluable wheat and salt were spoiled. The colonists had perhaps twenty days of food left, and it was now too late to plant crops. Another pilot quickly sailed away to try and capture fishing boats in Newfoundland. It became ever more clear that the islands had no

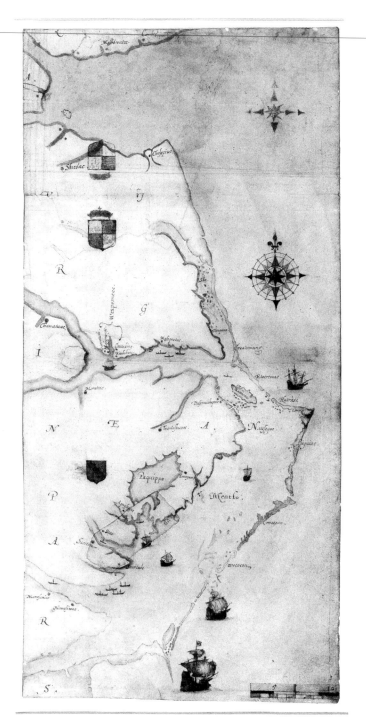

John White's map of the Roanoke voyages. Roanoke is the island near the ship that is farthest up the coastline. The large ship near the bottom is probably the Tiger.

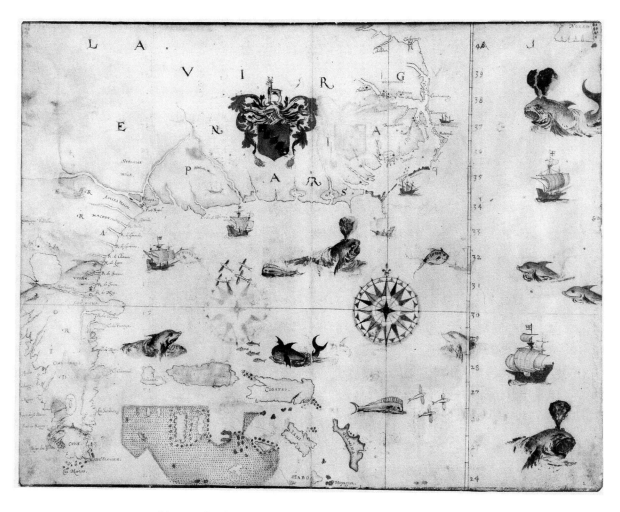

On this second White map, Port Ferdinando has been added near an inlet in the Outer Banks, right next to the ship to the left of the number 37. The coat of arms, which matches his seal, is Ralegh's.

John White's drawing of the well-organized village of Secoton. Secoton appears on his first map (page 66) in the lower quarter of the page, just inland from the two ships and four row boats, near what is now the Pamlico River.

ports deep enough for large ships and thus offered no good defense against the Spanish. In an exposed position with little food, the English could risk leaving only a small crew.

Before he returned to England to get more supplies, Grenville helped Lane scout the terrain. As the English fanned out, they learned more about how the natives lived. To White this was a wonderful opportunity, and the drawings he made of a village named Secoton are the best record we have of life in America before the arrival of the English. But when a silver cup disappeared and the natives who were thought to have it fled, a party led by Amadas destroyed their grain and burned their village. This was a bad sign. It was a forecast of the harsh and violent tone of the new settlement. Still, in late July, Manteo and a chieftain who had met Amadas a year earlier invited the English to stay on Roanoke Island.

By early September all the ships left, taking samples of local products including tobacco and sketch maps of the islands. On its way back the *Tiger* swung by Bermuda and captured a rich Spanish merchant ship named the *Santa Maria*. This prize was the fleet's only real success. Its cargo of ginger and sugar, as well as jewels taken from the crew, gave Ralegh and his fellow investors a decent profit. The first results were clear: American colonies were a bad risk, while buccaneering could be a great investment.

THE FIRST COLONY: IRELAND IN AMERICA

The first English colony in America consisted of Lane and his 108 men. All the others had left out of fear or because there was not enough food to sustain them. Lane had made his reputation in Ireland defending the new plantations. His model of how to deal with conquered, "primitive" peoples was the harsh English rule in Ireland. Experienced at using force to deal with hesitant chiefs or untrustworthy allies, he had no interest in making alliances with the natives. He was running a frontier garrison. Another man in his position might have created a different model for American history. But he was also hardworking, tough, and decisive. Under another leader the colonists might not have made it through the winter.

The colony was especially vulnerable because of the attitude of the wealthier men. According to Hariot, "Some also were of a nice bringing up, only in cities or towns, or such as never (as I may say) had seen the world before. Because there were not to be found any English cities, nor such fair houses, nor . . . any of their old accustomed dainty food, nor any soft beds of down or feathers, the country was to them miserable." Such men saw America as a chance for a quick fortune. If it did not provide that particular type of El Dorado, they were ready to go home.

What wealth might the new lands hold? Gold was an obvious hope, but no one thought there was too much chance of finding any large amount. Copper, though, seemed a realistic possibility, especially when the English were told an elaborate story of how the coastal people came to have it. One major mission of Lane's group was to go on an expedition in search of copper. A good part of the success of the entire settlement rested on the results of that search.

When Lane's record of the trip was published in 1589, he explained just how important a good mine was to the future of English settlement in America. "The discovery of a good mine, by the goodness of God, or a passage to the South Sea, or some way to it, and nothing else can bring this country in request to be inhabited by our nation." The contrast between

Chesapeake
Bay

RALEGH'S
VIRGINIA

Skicoac

VIRGINIA

*ATLANTIC
OCEAN*

Chawanoac
(Lane visits,
March 1586)

Chowan R.

Lane
explores,
1586

Albermarle Sound

Roanoke R.

Roanoke Island
Colonies of
1585-6, 1587-?

Port Ferdinando

Hatarask Island
(Barlow & Amadas
land, 1584)

Aquascogoc   Pomeioc

Pamlico Sound

Croatoan
Island

Drake anchors,
1586

Wococon Inlet

Cape
Lookout

Scale of 50 miles

Lane and Barlowe shows two very different ways Europeans viewed America: one a wary, tough-minded soldier and the other a salesman eager to promote new colonies.

To Lane, the wonderful climate and the abundant crops of America would not draw any English inhabitants unless there was a very specific and powerful goal to lure them there: a mine, or a passage to the East. Even the soil, he realized, needed to be fertilized. Virginia was nothing like the abundant, almost mythic land Barlowe advertised. Instead, it was raw land that had to be mastered, mined, and used.

Lane differed in his opinion of the natives, too. Over the course of the winter and spring he came to suspect, and probably actually to detect, hostility and even a real threat in the behavior of Wingina, a powerful chief.

When the English learned that Wingina was about to attack them, they in turn planned their own surprise raid. In the fight Wingina was injured but managed to flee into the woods. Edward Nugent, an Irish soldier, took off after him. Soon Nugent returned in triumph, holding the chieftain's severed head in his hand.

Who was the "savage"? The Irish soldier fighting for his life? The English captain protecting his men? The chief, struggling to hold off intruders who were consuming his corn and attacking his people? Maybe it was their blind contacts, so fraught with misunderstanding, that made savages of them all.

A few months after this battle, a relief fleet led by Sir Francis Drake finally arrived. It came to reprovision the men. But when terrible storms began to rage, Drake and Lane decided that it was too dangerous for the ships to remain. The best offer they could make was to take the bedraggled men home. On June 18, 1586, the ships sailed with all the English on board, save for three who were away from the ship. In the hurry and confusion, it is also possible that several of the South American natives and black slaves Drake had freed from the Spanish escaped on shore.

This was the legacy of Lane's men: no mine, no sweet Golden Age Indians, no cargo, nothing but armed exploration and fighting. Even the local black pearls carefully strung together as a perfect gift for the queen were lost in the crush to get away. It would take a very large mind to see beyond this history of hostility and failure. Fortunately there were two such men in the colony: Hariot took extensive notes and wrote a long report, parts of which have survived, matched with paintings by White. These words and images described exactly the same land as Lane and Barlowe did and yet came to startlingly different conclusions.

An Ingenious People

White's painting of a chieftain, surely Wingina, and Hariot's notes show a man they valued very highly. Hariot describes a time when Wingina came to "pray and sing psalms," to share in their devotions. To Hariot, Wingina was not an enemy; he was a potential friend.

His notes show how deep this admiration ran and where it stopped: "In their proper manner, considering the want of such means as we have, they seem very ingenious. For although they have no such tools, nor any such crafts, sciences and arts as we, yet, in those things they do, they show excellency of wit."

While Lane's men saw the Americans as enemies to be defeated or primitives to be conquered, Hariot was interested in their achievements. He could

*White's drawing of a person
thought to be Wingina.*
(COURTESY THE BRITISH MUSEUM)

put aside his prejudices and appreciate the talent and intelligence of people who must have seemed quite strange to him. He went past seeing easy differences to being curious about hidden similarities. We can see just how great a leap he took in one breathtaking comment.

Wingina and other chiefs faced difficult decisions about how to relate to the English. One key question was whether they were people at all rather than gods, demons, or reincarnated spirits. The fact that the strangers did not seem to need women and owned amazing tools and weapons suggested that they might be inhuman. The most powerful argument for this was their ability to kill without weapons. Neither natives nor English understood infectious diseases, such as smallpox, to which the Europeans had acquired some immunity but which were deadly to people who had never been exposed to them. As a result, neither could explain the sudden sickening and death that followed the arrival of the settlers.

Hariot learned that some natives thought the deaths were a "special work of God" on behalf on the English. That immediately made him think of how the English explained unusual things to themselves. For example, when there was an eclipse of the sun, "some Astrologers" thought it was "very terrible." These learned men were equally sure that "a comet which began to appear" predicted an outbreak of illness that broke out days later.

Hariot recognized that the English conviction that signs in the heavens showed divine judgment and the natives' belief that the English were supernatural were exactly equal. Both peoples explained the inexplicable by invoking gods and spirits. Instead of using American superstition to confirm English superiority, he held it up as a mirror to his own people.

Hariot and White were curious about the new lands and willing to question their own beliefs; in this, they were totally different from almost every other settler before or since. Hariot's notes and White's art are marvels of evenhanded clarity. The Americans are neither made into mythological innocents nor seen as horrible savages; instead, they go about their own lives by their own sensible rules.

Still, there was a limit to the open-mindedness of the English. Hariot assumed that the natives would recognize the advantages of English knowledge and religion, submit to instruction, and accept being "civilized" by the newcomers in their midst. This was exactly the model for the English conquests in Ireland and for the later British Empire. It is also precisely what the ex-colonies rejected in the twentieth century when they fought for their independence. It did not occur to Hariot—nor was it plausible—to argue that the Europeans should leave the Americans alone.

Which America did Ralegh support: the Golden Age place of myth, the jumping-off point for some profitable buccaneering, the staging area for economic surveys and military conquest, or the meeting place of different but equally important human beings? All of these. Each one of these beliefs reflected a side of his complex personality. If the legacy of his missions to America was Barlowe's glowing report, Grenville's prize ship, or Lane's grim battles, it was also Hariot's and White's humble and humane studies. All these views came together again in Ralegh's repeated efforts to find an El Dorado across the seas in the New World.

Chapter 7

DREAMS AND MIRAGES

In the late 1580s Ralegh seemed to be on the verge of great success in three different places: America, Ireland, and the court of the queen. Whether by colonization, plantation, or royal decree, before long he would become a great lord. Yet in each place he was also in danger of losing all he had risked. Was he carefully tending three realistic dreams or, like Don Quixote after him, chasing after three mirages? No one, not even Sir Walter, could be sure.

When reports started to filter back from America, Ralegh had to weigh them carefully. After all, he was the one sending one crew after the other out across the sea. After considering both the ominous warnings and the glowing descriptions of America, Ralegh plunged on. He was not scared off by Lane's failure to find a mine. There was just too much promise across the ocean to resist. Instead, he set out to establish a city with his own name as the anchor of a new colony. He even commissioned shields for the men who would govern it.

The city was to be in a new location. Poring over maps with Hariot and White, Ralegh learned about the most promising discovery to come out of Lane's failed expedition. The English had found a much more appealing site for a colony, what we now call the Chesapeake Bay. It offered a deep harbor where large ships could land. According to a captured Spanish document, this wide waterway might even connect up with a sea that opened out to the Pacific. Even if it did not, the queen had officially given license to privateering (legalized piracy) against Spanish ships, and a safe harbor well up the Atlantic coast was an excellent home base for those raids. Finally, there was good reason to believe that copper, and perhaps even gold, could be found nearby.

The Chesapeake region seemed to be the answer to everyone's New World dreams, even White's and Hariot's. The natives there spoke an entirely different language from that of Wingina and his people. It is just possible that the Chesapeake leaders in the village of Skicoac actually invited Hariot and White to return with a settlement of men, women, and children that would grow alongside their own community.

Ralegh had one final reason to pick a new site for his new colony. On an expedition in August of 1586 Grenville had left fifteen men on Roanoke Island. He did not know that all of the other men had left. When Grenville returned to England, he may well have reported that the place looked barren and unpromising.

According to Manteo's people, who lived nearby at Croatoan, thirteen of the fifteen men Grenville left behind were attacked and fled in a small boat. That makes them lost colonists. Similarly, no one knows what became of the

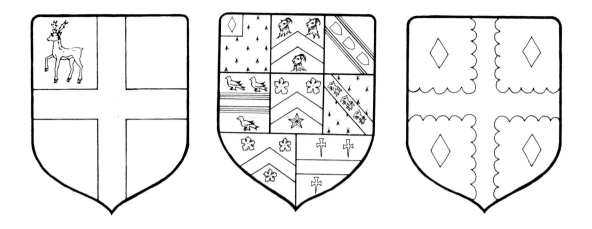

Heraldic shields prepared for the City of Ralegh and its leading families.

mixed group of men, possibly including Africans, South Americans, and English, left behind in Drake's hurried exit. People kept arriving at the narrow sandbars of the Outer Banks and disappearing from history.

Ralegh was optimistic about the new site. But he was too careful a planner and too ambitious a man to limit his hopes to a colony beyond the horizon. Even while he planned the next expedition to the New World, he used all his guile and influence to become a great lord in the Old.

An El Dorado in Ireland

After Ralegh left Ireland, the struggle in the southern part of the island continued. By late 1583 it was over. The English defeated and executed the rebellious Earl of Desmond. Throughout the large county of Munster, castles, church buildings, towns, and homes were destroyed, leaving only

Ralegh contemplates the world. The writing on the painting indicates he is thirty-six and that it was painted in 1588. This painting is thought to be a copy of an earlier original.

stones and brambles. Most of the local population was dead, dying of disease, or in flight. A region where the Irish had counted their wealth in cattle was now inhabited only by those that thrive in desolate wastes—wolves, foxes, and birds.

Although Ralegh played no part in this final devastation, he may have helped plan what the English would do with the ruined lands. If Ireland was to be of any value, the English had to plant it with English folk. And these needed to be organized and led by farseeing, ambitious men who believed in overseas colonies and settlements. Who could be better suited for this job than Sir Walter Ralegh, veteran Irish fighter and colonizer extraordinaire?

In February of 1587 Ralegh got his Irish bonanza. He requested and was granted provisional title to 42,000 acres of good land in the counties of Cork and Waterford. This was more than three times the legal size for any such grant. In exchange he was required to take over English people to farm and protect this land from either rebellious Irish or invading Spanish forces. Many of the people Ralegh took to Ireland were from Devon, which gave him a new way to pay back his local allies. If these loyal neighbors prospered, Ralegh, the son of a gentleman farmer, would be one of the richest and most powerful men in England.

Only a day's sail from England, Ireland seemed to offer Ralegh everything he wanted. But it did not. For the American voyages he was acting on his own, and that made him essentially the sovereign lord of whatever settlements were planted there. However much Ralegh, White, and Hariot respected the natives, no one had any interest in their beliefs about rights to the land. The Irish estates were granted by the government, and even though most Irish had left or lost legal title to their land, over time a nasty tangle of lawsuits brought into question exactly who owned what. Ralegh got more than anyone else in Ireland, and he tended to win court battles because he was in such high favor. But he could lose everything if he were not.

While involved in one particularly annoying suit, Ralegh wrote to his cousin Sir George Carew, "If in Ireland they think I am not worth the respecting, they shall much deceive themselves. I am in place to be believed not inferior to any man, to pleasure or displeasure the greatest; and my opinion is so received and believed as I can anger the best of them." Here was what some saw as Ralegh's arrogance: He would say what he wanted to anyone and bend whatever rules he needed to. Yet this was the bravado of a man whose entire worth rested on how highly his opinions were "received and believed" by the queen. Ireland was one more case where Ralegh was reaching for great power in a way that only confirmed how powerless he really was.

In the end Ralegh's vast estates in Ireland proved to be a burden, and they took up much of his time just when his American colony disappeared from sight. His most enduring legacy in Ireland may have been the introduction of one special tuber from the New World, the potato.

By 1602 Ralegh sold everything he owned in Ireland. He saw the island only twice after that, at the beginning and end of his final voyage in search of El Dorado. For Ralegh Ireland was but a way station to golden dreams.

CAPTAINS AND MAIDS

When Elizabeth appointed Ralegh as the captain of the guard in February of 1587, it was a great honor. In the hothouse atmosphere of her court of love, he was one of the most dazzling and gallant men. Now, like a cross between a husband and a bodyguard, he was directly responsible for keeping her from harm. As captain he also chose the guards, who were to be especially handsome young men. Ralegh was no longer the awkward, ardent suitor who threw his cape before the queen. Instead, he was her beloved old flame and needed to surround her with the kind of young man he once was.

Being captain of the guard hardly paid anything except in glory. But there was a side benefit that was a kind of parallel to Ralegh's role in finding men to please the eyes of the queen. The captain spent a lot of time with the ladies-in-waiting who served Elizabeth. Ralegh enjoyed to the fullest the endless opportunity for flirtation this created. In a sense he and the queen carried out their romance through these young men and women. Elizabeth was a jealous woman and did not want her men to love others. But in the crisscrossing of love notes, marriage suits, secret meetings, gifts, rumors, and affairs, could one always tell which beautiful words were directed to which beautiful woman or man?

Love for the queen, love for her ladies—this was the court of love in which Ralegh made his way. He'd tell Elizabeth in one poem that "when I found my self to you was true / I loved myself, because my self loved you." Then in a note pressed into a lady's pocket he urgently pleaded, "Would God thou knew the depth of my desire!" In turn, even as Elizabeth placed her life in Ralegh's hands, she turned her own attention ever more to Robert Devereux, the young, highborn, handsome, and passionate Earl of Essex.

When Essex came to court in 1584 as the eighteen-year-old stepson of the Earl of Leicester—Elizabeth's former swain Robert Dudley—the queen was already fifty-two years old. Tall, strikingly handsome, of noble blood, he was impetuous in a way she found both maddening and fascinating. By

The Earl of Essex.
(COURTESY THE NATIONAL PORTRAIT GALLERY, LONDON)

May of 1585 one court gossip whispered that "when she is abroad, nobody near her but my Lord of Essex, and at night my Lord at cards, or one game or another with her, that he cometh not to his lodgings till birds sing in the morning."

Essex was Ralegh's opposite. Sir Walter was an outsider who had risen on his wit and charm, while Essex was of ancient royal lineage. Essex was a popular hero, a charismatic soldier people loved to see on parade. To a fault, he rewarded his friends with titles and plunder. Many saw him as almost a king, who might take, or be given, the crown. Ralegh was an old court favorite who angered everyone with his pride and arrogant intelligence. No one liked Ralegh, but all feared him. Everyone liked Essex, but people feared being on the wrong side when he met his fate, whether on the throne or in rebellion against the queen.

Essex's first royal mission, bringing aid to the embattled French Protestants, revealed everything appealing and flawed in his character. He cut a fine figure when he was led into one city by six pages he had outfitted in bejeweled orange velvet with gold braid. And he showed his infectious charm when he beat the French king in a leapfrog contest. But he failed in battle. The contrast between Ralegh's grim experiences as a teenager fighting in France and Essex's boyish yet glamorous high jinks shows the difference in the two men.

When Elizabeth said Essex's performance had been "rather a jest than a victory," Essex defended himself like a true suitor. "The two windows of your Privy Chamber," he assured her seductively, "shall be the poles of my sphere, where, as long as your Majesty will please to have me, I am fixed and immovable."

Essex was the same kind of favorite as Ralegh, only younger, more handsome, and of noble blood. And for all the estates the queen kept presenting to Ralegh and the honors she gave him, she never made him a lord or placed him on the council of her closest advisers.

Perhaps even as he whispered one more sweet rhyme in the queen's ear, Ralegh sensed that the whole dance would one day end. Christopher Marlowe, the great playwright and a friend of Ralegh's, wrote a famous poem about courtship. The entire theme of his "The Passionate Shepherd to His Love" is "Come live with me, and be my love;/And we will all the pleasures prove." It is a poem in praise of birdsong, roses, May mornings, and the delights that come from seizing a moment's pleasure. Ralegh wrote a response, "The Nymph's Reply to the Shepherd," which takes the long view of what happens after those golden moments pass:

> *If all the world and love were young,*
> *And truth in every shepherd's tongue,*
> *These pretty pleasures might me move*
> *To live with thee, and be thy love.*

But flowers fade, spring turns to winter, sweet sounds ebb into silence, and youth grows old. The mature captain to an aging queen was still a captain. The favorite courtier now having to vie with a younger suitor was still in high favor. Yet Ralegh may well have seen winter coming in the full light of spring.

Chapter 8

THE NEW HOPE
AND THE TERRIBLE YEAR

While Ralegh hoped his plantations in Ireland or America would give him enough wealth and power to enter the nobility, John White had more humble aims. He had risen a small way in English society on his skill as a painter. He knew the dreams and frustrations of people whose best hope for bettering themselves is to develop a craft. White's image of a New World colony looks ahead to the America we know today.

His plan was to gather together families, most probably from London, who would sell everything they owned and pay their own way to America. These would not be hired men, like those who had served under Lane. They would be free people who put up their own money and who would find their own ways to turn a profit. This was the ideal of America as a land of opportunity, much like the "golden door" later celebrated at the Statue of Liberty.

Just at this point in the spring and summer of 1587 as White, his pregnant daughter and her husband, their fellow colonists, and their now quite English ally Manteo set to sea in the *Lion,* the story grows more confusing. Their pilot was that old salt Simon Fernandez, whom we last saw paired with Grenville as more pirate than explorer. Fernandez kept taking unexplained detours through the Caribbean that infuriated White. The motivation was simple: privateering. This was such a usual part of any voyage that White should have expected it. Instead, he grew ever more hostile to his pilot and ever less able to take command of his mission.

When he left the Caribbean, Fernandez took the *Lion* to Roanoke Island, which was reasonable enough, since it gave White a chance to look for the men Grenville had left behind. White then planned to "pass along the coast to the Bay of 'Chesepiok' where we intended to make our seat and fort according to the charge given us among other directions in writing under the hand of Sir Walter Ralegh." That is where the new colony was to be located. But Fernandez had other ideas. He claimed that he had to get back to privateering soon or there would be no good plunder that season. He was not willing to go on to the Chesapeake. The colony would have to make do for itself in Roanoke, or move on its own to a new location.

Why did the pilot dump his passengers? Was he a calculating villain secretly working for the Spanish, a greedy selfish raider, or a good Joe trying to protect the colony from the more aggressive and violent natives of the Chesapeake? But then, why didn't White have any authority over his pilot? Could he not have insisted on being taken that much farther up the coast? We will probably never know. All we can be sure of is that by late July the English were back on Roanoke Island. And in August Manteo became a Christian and was installed as the leader of his people in the region. If the settlers were in a bad spot, they at least seemed to have a nearby and powerful ally.

On August 18, 1587, White's daughter Elenor and her husband, Anias Dare, became parents of a daughter. Six days later, at her christening, White wrote, "because this child was the first Christian born in Virginia, she was named Virginia." Virginia Dare was the first English Protestant child born in North America. She was a sign of hope for the new kind of colony into which she was born. The city of Ralegh would bring new life and perhaps a new way of life to the world.

Still, White's colonists faced a crisis. Ralegh and all the colony's allies in England expected them to be in the Chesapeake region, which was where their sponsors would send supplies and new colonists. But they were stuck on Roanoke Island, where previous settlers had fought with natives, and they knew it would be hard to find enough food to make it through the winter. The only answer was to send a spokesman back to England, who would quickly gather together a relief expedition. The one man who they were sure would do the job was John White. He had led them to America, and he would do everything in his power to bring back help from England. Very reluctantly White agreed. On August 27 he left, bearing every hope for his colony and every fear for his young family.

White tried very hard for the next three years to sail back and to save the colony. The single largest obstruction he faced was England's war with Spain. Once the friction between those two powers turned to actual fighting, and especially to battles at sea, there was no way anyone could return to America. The colony that meant so much to White, and to American history, was meaningless to anyone in power in Europe.

THE ARMADA

As the great and terrible year of 1588 neared, the predictions of the seer Regiomontanus, elaborated and confirmed by an army of scholars, astrologers, and scribblers, spread across all Europe. The turning point in human history was about to arrive.

Johann Müller was a mathematician in the fifteenth century. His tables of the stars helped navigators from Columbus on to find their way. Under the name of Regiomontanus, though, he was something else: a prophet who could divine the future. In the lines of star charts Regiomontanus discovered that in one dire year there would be an eclipse of the sun followed by two total eclipses of the moon, as well as a conjunction of three planets: Saturn, Jupiter, and Mars. Surely 1588 would be a fateful year. He wrote:

> *A thousand years after the virgin birth*
> *and after five hundred more allowed the globe,*
> *the wonderful eighty-eighth year begins and*
> *brings with it woe enough. If, this year,*
> *total catastrophe does not befall, if land*
> *and sea do not collapse in total ruin, yet*
> *will the whole world suffer upheavals, empires*
> *will dwindle and from everywhere will*
> *be great lamentation.*

One spy for the Vatican in England sent back a confirmation of Regiomontanus's warning. Apparently a wondrous discovery had just come to light in the ruins of fabled Glastonbury Abbey. An ancient marble slab suddenly appeared, and miraculously inscribed on it was the exact same prophecy. It must have lain there hidden and undisturbed since Merlin's day. The rule of the heirs of Uther Pendragon was about to end; the true Arthur would return with the true religion. The skeptical cardinal who read this report added just one question: Next to the line "empires will dwindle" he wrote, "It doesn't say which empires or how many."

This was exactly what Hariot realized: Europeans looking in the sky saw portents that made them the center of God's plans. But which empire would fall? Which side would God favor, Catholic Spain or Protestant England? For decades both had been using diplomacy, intrigue, plot, and sea battles to jockey for position. Now they were finally about to go to war, to holy war. Clearly the prophecies about 1588 all pointed to this Armageddon, this final struggle of Christian kingdoms.

Philip II of Spain thought of astrology as pagan, sacrilegious. He was fighting for God, not to fulfill a prophecy. And he had his own special strategy. He would send the largest fleet ever seen on earth to challenge the nimble English ships. Once in control of the English Channel, his grand Armada would join with the fighters Protestants feared most: the battle-tested warriors who had fought so ferociously in the Netherlands under the Duke of Parma. Their naval power broken, their homeland invaded by merciless and disciplined troops, the English would surely accept defeat. For the many Catholics and secret Catholics throughout England and Ireland, this would not even be a defeat; it would be a liberation from Protestant tyranny.

Elizabeth possessed nowhere near the money or manpower to invade Spain. And if the Armada defeated her ships, she would lose her life and her kingdom, which might well mean the complete destruction of her Protestant faith. Her sole aim was to survive, not to conquer. But the one thing the English did very well was the one approach that might work: They could endlessly attack and harass the lumbering Spanish ships until the discouraged fleet broke up and went home.

When the Armada was about to set off, the leader of the fleet held a special ceremony. On April 25, 1588, a man with the grand name and titles of Don Alonso Pérez de Guzmán, el Bueno Duque de Medina-Sidonia, Captain General of Andalusia, Captain General of the Ocean Sea, went to the cathedral in Lisbon. Every one of the twenty thousand soldiers and eight thousand sailors under his command confessed and took communion. The archbishop of Lisbon said Holy Mass and blessed the venture. Then the standard of the expedition was shown to the men. The banner showed the crucified Jesus on the front and the Virgin Mary on the back. In Latin it blazed forth the words of David in the Psalms: "Arise, O Lord, and vindicate thy cause."

In England there was no such ceremony, although there was some very similar thinking. When Elizabeth asked her vice admiral, the savvy captain Sir Francis Drake, how he intended to beat the Armada, he answered: "There was never any force so strong as there is ready or making ready against your Majesty and true religion; but . . . the word of the Lord of all strengths is stronger and will defend the truth of his word."

Both sides trusted in God. But they were also extremely sober and practical men. In private a special representative of the pope cornered one of the leaders of the Armada and asked him to tell the truth: Were they going to win this war? The officer assured him they would. The papal delegate was not convinced and pushed harder. How could the officer be sure?

It is very simple. It is well known that we fight in God's cause. So, when we meet the English, God will surely arrange matters so that we can grapple and board them, either by sending some strange freak of weather or, more likely, just by depriving the English of their wits. If we can come to close quarters, Spanish valour and Spanish steel (and the great masses of soldiers we shall have on board) will make our victory certain. But unless God helps us by a miracle the English, who have faster and handier ships than ours, and many more long-range guns, and who know their advantage just as well as we do . . . will . . . stand aloof and knock us to pieces without our being able to do them any serious hurt. . . . We are sailing against England in the confident hope of a miracle.

The captain's assessment of his opponent was perfect. The Invincible Armada, as it came to be called, was massive. Among its 131 ships were 20 galleons, the battleships of the day; 4 galleasses, fast, deadly, sailing ships that slaves could row when there was no wind; 4 massive merchant ships bristling with cannon; 40 smaller but also armed merchant ships; and a wide array of other craft to help with supplies, men, and transport. Philip II was the richest and most powerful ruler in the world, which is why he could pay for so many ships, sailors, soldiers, cannon, ammunition, and supplies. Still, the entire fate of the Armada depended on fighting the old-fashioned kind of battle the Spanish had mastered.

The English were determined to make sure that would not happen. For ten years with Ralegh's active and enthusiastic support Sir John Hawkins had been laboring to rethink the English warship so that it could fight a new kind of naval battle. He built or refitted ships so that they could carry more ship-destroying guns and sail closer to the wind than anything in the sea. He took down the high "castles" that stood on the bows and sterns of existing galleons, since they could hold only the light guns suited to close combat. Hawkins's ships were faster, more maneuverable, and better able to strike from a distance than any ships in history.

The Spanish needed to fling their grappling irons across the English hulls so that they could fight hand to hand from deck to deck. The English could win only if they rested at a safe distance, blasting the wooden galleons with the largest cannon ever seen at sea. While the English stayed out of range of Spanish muskets and swords, the unrelenting fire of their culverins and demiculverins would rip the Spanish ships apart.

We do not know exactly what Ralegh did during this epochal combat. He must have desperately yearned to be part of the action. He was unflinchingly brave, a seasoned sailor; he knew how to fight the Spanish and, like Drake, was eager to take on the enemy no matter what the odds. With its special rigging (topgallants that unfurled above the main and topsails), four masts instead of three, and its cannon on either side of the rudder, his own ship the *Ark Ralegh* was the best of the new-style galleons. But the queen gave him a special responsibility that most likely kept him on shore for the duration. Lord Howard, the admiral of the English fleet, used Ralegh's ship for himself.

In 1587 Ralegh had joined the great council of war that planned for the coming combat. Named as lieutenant general of Cornwall, he was placed in charge of organizing the first line of defense against the expected invasion. He had to find, train, and deploy soldiers and cavalry at key points in Devon and Cornwall. If the Spanish beat the English in the water, or even if they landed small units of soldiers here and there, Ralegh needed to figure out how to use untrained men to defeat the toughest troops in Europe in the warfare they knew best.

The Ark Ralegh. (COURTESY THE BRITISH MUSEUM)

On July 19, 1588, a sharp-eyed scout lit a beacon on the far scraggly coast of England that is called the Lizard. He had sighted the first ship of the dreadful crescent: the battle formation of the Invincible Armada. From flame to flame the news spread in a carefully orchestrated relay, probably put in place by Ralegh. Smoke curled over the headlands as each new flare passed the warning along. Soon the whole coast, across to Dover and then up to London and north to York, knew that the battle was about to begin.

The Armada's crescent was a perfect expression of the Spanish approach to war. It took unprecedented planning and coordination to make so many

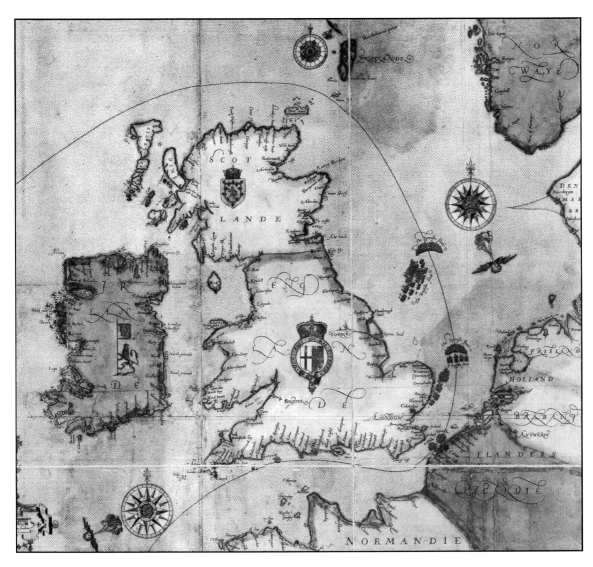

A map of the battle, showing the moving crescent of Spanish ships and the English arrayed against it. Note the clash involving the hellburners just off the coast of France.

ships work together. And the effect was terrifying. The deadliest galleons were on the wings. They would engage the enemy. If any unfortunate ship tried to escape, it would be pulled in, like a helpless insect sucked into the maw of a Venus flytrap. This massive funnel of destruction was now sweeping down the channel, always in full sight of the English people watching from the shore.

During the first four days of what proved to be a nine-day battle, the ships moved along the coastline Ralegh was sworn to protect. Moving parallel to the fleet, he and his troops watched closely, listening to every report, rushing to defend each port where the Spanish might land. But the Spanish did not make for Plymouth, or Portland, or even the Isle of Wight. The Armada was constantly frustrated by the nimble English boats that managed to stay ahead of the shifting winds while peppering their ships with cannon fire. The English in turn were astonished by the steady control of the fabulous crescent. Though they could rake an exposed ship with cannon fire, none of their shots did significant damage. Long-range cannon were proving to be something like modern-day bombing from the air: a strategy that looks devastating on paper but is never quite as effective in practice.

Each side, though, had an ultimate weapon. For the Spanish it was essential that the Armada join up with the Duke of Parma's troops. His land invasion was the key to everything. By July 27 the Armada reached the coast off the French port of Calais. It could rest there near friendly shores and join up with Parma's men. The English had to roust the great fleet out of its harbor and push it back to sea. They had done everything to avoid direct confrontation. What could they do now? In a council of war the British decided to use their most fearsome weapon: fireboats.

Setting a ship aflame and letting it loose in the path of an enemy is an ancient tactic. Before they sailed, the Spanish heard that a much more deadly variation had just been invented. An Italian engineer named Federigo Giambelli had created a new kind of fireboat with an apt name: the hellburner. Hellburners were more bombs than ships, for once lit, they would not merely burn but explode, taking a wide circle of ships with them. Giambelli was known to be in England. And the Spanish could see mysterious small boats sailing to the English fleet. Perhaps these were Giambelli's ultimate weapons.

It must have been a horrifying sight: in the darkness of midnight, July 28, first one, then two, then six, then eight orange balls of flame blooming on the English side, then gliding across the water. The hellburners, the unmanned guided missiles of their day, sailed steadily across the water toward the Spanish fleet. The Armada's whole strategy was based on close coordination, acting as one. Now unstoppable terror was coming their way, and the only hope was to cut anchor and scatter.

Truth to tell, there were no hellburners. That was nothing but rumor. These were conventional fireships with only a slight variation. The English filled them with loaded guns that fired when their iron burned white hot. Still, the spray of shot from arms manned by ghosts may have been just enough to confirm Spanish fears.

Hellburners as fact and as rumor were a terrible blow to the Spanish, but the game was already lost. Parma never made it to the rendezvous. There were no troops to pick up. The Armada failed to make possible the great invasion of England. Now all it had to do was sail home, to make ready to fight another day.

Looking back, Ralegh shifted around some of the facts and was typically contemptuous. He also left out the force that finally destroyed the Invincible Armada.

> Their navy, which they termed invincible . . . were by thirty of Her Majesty's own ships of war, and a few of our merchants . . . beaten and shuffled together, even from the Lizard in Cornwall, first to Portland . . . from Portland to Calais . . . and from Calais . . . were chased out of sight of England, round about Scotland and Ireland.

The strength of the English navy is not what did the real damage. As the Spanish Armada entered the North Sea, it was battered by storms that turned the invasion from failure to rout. Fifty-six ships and thousands of lives were lost. When the English struck a medal to commemorate their victory, it read, "God blew his winds and they were scattered." In a sense Philip agreed. He wrote, "I sent my ships to fight against men and not against the winds and waves of God." "Even kings," he added with sincere piety, "must submit to being used by God's will without knowing what it is."

With the distance of four hundred years, we can look at the fate of the Armada without assuming that God was on either side. Yet there was something about the differences between Catholicism and Protestantism that was reflected in the battle. No European navy before the Armada was ever so large and so well coordinated from one central command. In that sense it was like the single, universal, and hierarchical Catholic Church with one person at its center. Catholic Spain was the first empire in world history to circle the globe. Its possessions and ports ringed the Asian Pacific, covered key parts of Europe, spread across South America, and extended well into what are now Florida and California. To manage such a far-flung empire required a level of organization, structure, and attention to detail that had never been seen before. The close-order crescent bearing down on the straggly line of English ships was an apt symbol of Philip, of Spain, and of the Catholic Church.

Aside from their ships, the English had two things going for them. They were fighting close to home, so it was easy for them to resupply their ships, and their best sailors knew every tide, shoal, current, and rock. Then there was their training. England never possessed the wealth or strength to fight a full-scale battle against Spain. Instead, until war became almost inevitable, Elizabeth could only pretend not to know when the best captains went to sea to seek Spanish prizes. These tough sailors had to act on their own, with no possible protection from the queen. This made them all the more inventive and resilient.

If Catholicism taught order, discipline, and structure, Protestantism stressed individual knowledge. This is roughly mirrored in the highly organized Spanish fleet versus the freebooting English buccaneers. We cannot take this too far, as Elizabeth was certainly devoted to hierarchy. The Anglican Church of her day did not tolerate much dissent, and it is easy to find examples of individual initiative on the Spanish side. Still, the Armada against the Sea Dogs, the crescent against the darting ships, was also the single-world empire against a land in which people had to make choices for themselves.

As the English Grand Fleet returned to port, Elizabeth was left with one last chore. The Spanish always hoped that secret Catholics in the English forces would rise in rebellion to support their cause. The queen needed to make sure that a victory at sea was also one at home. This she could achieve only by making a personal bond with her fighting men. The modern Diana, the warrior virgin, went down to meet the troops that had been assembled to defend England.

Riding a pure white horse and accompanied by the exquisitely handsome Earl of Essex, she toured the camp. Then she stopped to speak and gave one of the great speeches of her reign, and perhaps in all of English history. Elizabeth showed how a single woman could stand as the fighting lord of an embattled land. She swore that if anyone, even King Philip himself, dared to "invade the borders" of her realm, she would "take up arms" herself as England's "general." To riotous applause she declared that "I know I have the body of a weak and feeble woman, but I have the heart and stomach of a king, and of a king of England too." Who could fail to love such a queen?

Chapter 9

THE AGONY OF JOHN WHITE

easured against the clash of empires, John White's desperate need to get back across the Atlantic was a tiny annoyance. Certainly it meant nothing to Elizabeth. The city of Ralegh was her courtier's venture, not the government's. She lost nothing if the settlement failed, and she would get her share anyway if, by wild chance, the settlers succeeded in locating a good harbor or a rich mine. On October 9, 1587, in preparation for the coming war with Spain, Elizabeth had forbidden any ship to leave English ports.

Ralegh did care, and with his power and influence in Dover he could let a ship or two slip out to sea. White gathered some new colonists and waited for the signal to leave. By March of 1588 Grenville was ready to chance it with a small but tough squad of five privateering boats. They were the *Galleon Dudley*, the *Virgin God Save Her*, the *Tiger* (not the one he had taken to America in 1586), the *Golden Hind* (not Drake's), and the *St. Leger*. Bad winds held all of them in port until, on the last day of the month, Grenville was ordered to bring all the ships to Plymouth as part of the defense against the Armada.

War or not, Armada be damned, White was determined to get back across the sea. He switched his hopes to two ships that were too insignificant to matter to the English defense, a rather small craft called the *Brave* and an even smaller one named the *Roe*. Their size allowed them to escape naval duty. They would have little protection, however, from pirates or Spaniards.

On April 22, 1588, White and eleven hopeful colonists, perhaps including spouses of those already in America, set off in the two frail boats. Ralegh assured them that he would send more people and supplies as soon as he could. But even his wishes mattered little at sea. There the captain's law ruled. Once again the two captains were out for pirate gold and were in no rush to get to America. Within days they chased and boarded six boats. The *Roe*, a better craft, soon sped ahead and lost contact with its companion.

On May 5 disaster struck in the form of bigger and better pirates. A French ship overtook the *Brave* and blasted it with fire. White wrote that "I myself was wounded twice in the head, once with a sword and another time with a pike." Soon the ship was taken over, stripped of its goods and even many of its sails, and left to bob in the waves. White thought this was "God justly punishing our former thievery of our evil-disposed mariners." That may have been some spiritual comfort, but the reality was that they were "constrained to break off our voyage intended for the relief of the colony left the year before in Virginia."

White must have felt that he held the fate of the colony in his hands, so the delay was a bitter blow. But it is possible that he was too late already. Even as he struggled to leave England, a Spanish ship was sailing up the coast of America to scout out the "English settlement and fort." The Spaniards assumed this was located near the good harbors of the Chesapeake Bay, where a strong force would be a serious threat to their ships. Captain Vicente González traveled far enough to note the size of the Potomac and the large rocks guarding the entrance to the Susquehanna. He found few natives and no English. On his way back he noted that on Roanoke Island "there were signs of a slipway [boatyard] for small vessels, and on land a number of wells made with English casks, and other debris indicated that a considerable number of people had been here." This may mean that by June of 1588 the settlers had already left the island.

It might seem that the defeat of the Armada should have made it easy for White to cross the sea. But Elizabeth kept her ban on shipping. The English were still at war with the world's most powerful empire and did not want to take any unnecessary risks. Ralegh was more distracted than ever by Ireland and by the ebb and flow of his standing at court. Essex was by now not merely a rival but a real threat. The best Ralegh could do for White was to put him in touch with his backer, William Sanderson, and let the two of them find new ways to finance another expedition.

The solution White and Sanderson arrived at—a company organized to support the colony—was in many ways a model for what was later tried in Jamestown. Even with this backing, throughout 1589 White was unable to find men or ships willing to go to America. Privateering in the Caribbean was the only thing that battle-hardened sailors and sea-wise captains wanted to do. And after his experience on the *Brave,* he knew better than to sail into dangerous waters without a sturdy fleet of well-armed ships. Yet another year passed by with the fretting White in England. In 1587 he had been sent from America with the mandate to return quickly. As 1590 neared, he was entering the third year of helplessness and separation.

Finally Ralegh and Sanderson, with the aid of a privateering syndicate, put together enough ships to carry people and supplies to America and to provide protection through the Caribbean: the *Moonlight*, captained by White's friend Edward Spicer; the *Hopewell*, under the command of Abraham Cocke; the *Little John*, captained by Christopher Newport, who later took the colonists to Jamestown; and the *John Evangelist*, under the guidance of William Lane. At the last minute Cocke refused to take any colonists but White. Angry as he must have been, White could only agree. On March 20, 1590, he set sail to make good his most fervent promise.

There is one important relic of the fleet's trip across the sea and through the Caribbean. Somewhere between Mexico and Cuba Captain Newport caught a Spanish treasure boat. In the fighting he lost his right arm, and the captured ship was so damaged that it sank. A rotting hull with thirteen casks of Spanish silver is still there beneath the sea, waiting to be salvaged.

Finally, in mid-August, White reached the coast of Virginia. His eyes searched everywhere, eager for any hint of welcome. At first there was a very encouraging sign. Across the flat sea islands White and the others spied a great plume of white smoke rising into the sky. Could this be a signal from the colony? No, they soon realized, just a huge brushfire. That false hope must have been hard to take, but what followed was much worse.

On the morning of August 16, 1590, White, Cocke, and Spicer left their ships and headed for the Outer Banks in small rowboats. The waters were still choppy from a recent storm, and Captain Spicer's boat upended. He and some of his best men—who were also White's closest allies—drowned.

It took all of Cocke's and White's authority to keep the small crew that was left from returning to the ships. By this time darkness was making any movement dangerous, but the English had reached Roanoke Island, and they made one last effort to announce their arrival. They "sounded with a trumpet a call, & afterwards many familiar English tunes of songs . . . but we had no answer." Discouraged, they fell asleep in their boats. White was almost within sight of his goal, and yet he had to suffer one more delay.

The next day White finally reached the spot he had left nearly three years before. "We entered up the sandy bank, upon a tree, in the very brow thereof were curiously carved these fair Roman letters CRO." This was a code he could make out. "According to a secret token agreed between them and me at my last departure from them, which was that in any ways they should not fail to write or carve on the trees or posts of the doors the name of the place where they should be seated." Though they planned to go on to the Chesapeake, for some reason the colonists decided to move to Manteo's domain, to Croatoan.

This was a mixed message for White. There was no one on Roanoke Island to meet him, but he now knew where the colonists had gone, and he could assume they were safe. After all, when he left, "I willed them that if they should happen to be distressed in any of these places that they should carve over the letters a cross in this form ✚, but we found no such sign of distress." Both messages were confirmed when he came to the site where the houses of the colony once stood and saw "one of the chief trees or posts at the right side of the entrance had the bark taken off and 5 feet from the ground in fair capital letters was graven CROATOAN without any cross or sign of distress."

There was, though, one kind of evidence that was a very personal blow to White. Three of his own chests lay in ruins. "Many of my things spoiled and broken, and my books torn from their covers, the frames of some of my pictures and maps rotten and spoiled with rain, and my armor almost eaten through with rust." Even if the colony was safe, no one had cared that his most precious possessions were left behind to rot. Perhaps in those torn frames and rusted armor John White saw the death of his family and his dreams.

White's next move should have been simplicity itself. All he had to do was to visit his ally, the Christian, English-speaking ruler of Croatoan, Manteo, and he would at best find his family and friends, or at worst learn directly what had become of them. This, fate once again prevented him from doing.

The two ships that made it to the Outer Banks were the *Hopewell* and the *Moonlight*, and both were desperately short of fresh water. The *Hopewell*, battered by the weather, was barely seaworthy. The *Moonlight* had lost so many men that its captain would not let it take any more risks. Neither captain was willing to stay in America and wait for White to explore, or to take him up the coast in search of his colony.

The best Cocke could offer was to sail down to the Caribbean, resupply, and return in the spring. Even this plan failed when the *Hopewell*, with White on board, proved too damaged to make for Trinidad and instead set sail for the Azores. Finally, on October 24, 1590, White landed in England. He would never try to reach America again.

This is the most important sense in which the colony was lost: White lost hope. It was just too hard—too hard to fight backers for money and officials for clearances; too hard to battle captains over routes and priorities; too hard to risk bullets and cannon; too hard to weather wild hurricanes and suffer parching drought—all this for three chests rotting in an old trench, as dead and discarded as junkyard scrap.

Because no one reached Croatoan in time to ask Manteo about the English, it is left to us, at this great distance of time, to determine what became of them. The most thorough historian of the colony thinks the answer is in the messages White found. The colonists sent White back to England because they intended to move on to the Chesapeake. But the signs they carved on the trees stated clearly that they were headed for Croatoan. Why not assume that the colonists split up? One group could have set off for Skicoac, where they had reason to expect welcome. The rest might have gone to Croatoan under the protection of Manteo. This theory is reinforced by two kinds of later information: a confession from Powhatan, Pocahontas's father, and reports of gray eyes and English features in the Hatteras tribe that lived in various parts of North Carolina down through the 1730s.

Powhatan was a strong, determined, and militaristic chieftain. He put together a confederacy of peoples under his rule that dominated the Chesapeake region. From 1570 on, Europeans sailing into that bay had always met stiff resistance. That may have been why Fernandez refused to take the colonists there. The Powhatan were willing to use violence to protect their ground. The friendly people White and Hariot met at Skicoac were members of the only group Powhatan did not control.

According to Captain John Smith, Powhatan himself admitted what became of the colonists. In 1607, even as Captain Newport's ship carrying the Jamestown settlers neared its landing place, Powhatan's shamans warned him that his rule was about to end. To prevent that, he slaughtered all the English and part-English settlers he could find. Precisely because the colonists had survived and could pass on valuable information to the new-comers, he killed them all.

This could be true. But between Smith's tendency to put Powhatan in a bad light and the difficulty they must have faced in understanding each other, it is hard to be sure. It is a good reminder, though, of how much power the native Americans had over all of Ralegh's settlers. They provided the corn and fish that allowed the settlers to survive. Their protection was crucial to deciding if any plantation would take hold. And if they turned to war, they could overpower the small number of English on their shores. Until the natives were debilitated by disease, and until the English were willing and able to commit enough weaponry to overwhelm them, they controlled the fate of any visitors. No matter what Ralegh's patent said, Powhatan was the lord of his land.

There were fewer than ten Hatteras on the Outer Banks by the 1730s. Had anyone cared to listen to them, we might know much more. While there is no reason to doubt that they did have some foreign ancestors, these could have been of any race. Their forebears could have been any of the people who were abandoned on the islands beginning in the 1580s. And stray Spaniards had come to the region even before the English. The Hatteras's story is the reverse of Powhatan's: Once the European settlers with their African slaves defeated and drove off the Indians, they were pushed out of sight. No one asked much of the few remaining natives because no one wanted to know.

To the English the lost colony was a failed experiment. It failed because no single man, even one so powerful and determined as Ralegh, could overcome all the obstacles and plant a colony across the sea. Still, had he not been distracted by Ireland, war, and Essex, Ralegh might have realized that one of the New World products that he most enjoyed held the key to creating an enduring colony.

Jamestown succeeded because it enjoyed royal support, and, most importantly, because it developed a resource that was as valuable as a mine or a passage to the Pacific: tobacco. In 1613 the colony managed to grow just enough of the weed to send some back to England. Two years later two thousand pounds of cured leaves crossed the ocean. By 1617 twenty thousand pounds of valuable plants filled ships' stores, and two years after that sixty thousand. In Virginia, Lane was right and White was wrong. The hope of a new life was not a strong-enough draw to get people to keep crossing the sea when so many were sure to die. Only a very lucrative crop had that power.

What is the heritage that this tangled history leaves for us? Golden Age, golden land, golden door: These were the images of hope that brought people to America. Savagery, murder, betrayal, death: These were the results when peoples who were both too different and too similar got in each other's way. Between these high dreams and such nightmarish ends came one enduring result. White and Hariot left a unique record of another way of living on this planet. The legacy of the lost colony is art and understanding, not conquest.

El Dorado

Our natures do pursue,
Like rats that raven down their proper bane,
A thirsty evil; and when we drink, we die.

—William Shakespeare

Chapter 10

THE LIE

Sir Walter Ralegh rose by defying his enemies in battle, courting Elizabeth with sweet words and luminous pearls, and sending ships across the ocean "for gold, for praise, for glory." In return, the queen showered him with gifts. "Small drops of joys sweetened great worlds of woes." Even "her regal looks" could calm his "sighs." But the love Ralegh celebrated in the poem "The Book of the Ocean to Cynthia" rested on his absolute loyalty, and he wrote it precisely because she knew he was no longer true.

In 1592 court gossips began whispering that Ralegh had gotten one of the queen's ladies-in-waiting pregnant. Worse, he might even have married her. He denied this forcefully. But it was true. When Elizabeth Throckmorton gave birth to a son and then returned to court as if nothing had happened, her queen was furious. Not only had she been defied, she had been lied to and betrayed.

One witty court watcher saw what this could mean:

> The queen is most fiercely incensed, and . . . threateneth the most bitter punishment to both the offenders. S.W.R. will lose, it is thought, all his places and preferments at court . . . such will be the end of his speedy rising, and, now, he must fall as low as he was high, at which many will rejoice.

Ralegh's wealth and status came from the queen. Now his passion for another woman had eclipsed his love for his monarch. Elizabeth reacted as both a jealous lover and a vengeful ruler out to crush disloyalty. There was a good chance that she would take back everything she had given him. The great Sir Walter, who nearly gained title to much of North America, could well end up like his father, renting a farm in Devon.

In August Ralegh and his bride were placed under house arrest in Durham House. Cut off from the queen, Ralegh roiled in his own feelings: by turns desperate to regain her favor, terrified of how far he might fall, and angry with himself for ever having tried to rise. He began "Ocean to Cynthia" in an attempt to win Elizabeth back, but the more he wrote, the more his feelings raged out of control. "She is gone, she is lost. She is found, she is ever fair!" "Alone, forsaken, friendless" thoughts of his happier days burned "like flames of hell." Looking back at the campaign for the queen that had taken his entire adult life, Ralegh could only count the empty days: "Twelve years entire I wasted in this war."

Ralegh's world was collapsing. Not merely was he in danger of losing

Elizabeth Throckmorton. (COURTESY THE NATIONAL GALLERY OF IRELAND)

everything, his "damnable" pride and haughty arrogance were turning against him. People would laugh at his fall. The man who could disdain his enemies because he had the queen's favor was now at their mercy.

But Ralegh's enemies were not the only ones to criticize his years of living off the queen's favor. Looking back at the court with the clear eyes of a cynic, Ralegh himself saw how it was all a lie. In one startling poem, "The Lie," he stripped the covers off the entire world of illusions and deceptions in which he had made his home. To "give the lie" means to confront or expose, the way an examiner might force a suspect to face the truth.

> *Go soul the body's guest*
>   *upon a thankless errand,*
> *Fear not to touch the best*
>   *the truth shall be thy warrant:*
> *Go since I needs must die,*
>   *and give the world the lie.*

Set free, his soul shines a fearless light on the world, and shows its true colors:

> *Say to the Court it glows*
>   *and shines like rotten wood,*
> *Say to the Church it shows*
>   *what's good, and doth no good.*
> *If Church and Court reply,*
>   *then give them both the lie. . . .*

When the truth-telling spirit reaches the highest rulers, it reveals that they are loved solely because of the gifts they give. Who could fail to see Elizabeth in that image? Ministers are governed by ambition and "practice only hate." Schools care only about appearances, and lawyers just love to argue. Everything human is false, even love. Friendship is lost to "unkindness," love is just "lust," charity is defeated by "coldness," beauty is blasted by age, and what people call wisdom is hairsplitting and showing off.

In this unsparing poem Ralegh, the great courtier to the queen, showed the other side of his flattering, smiling face. For every bow he made at court, another voice cursed its "rot." The underside of the court of love, the glorious reign of the Virgin Queen, was cynicism, disgust, hypocrisy, and lies.

But not only lies. For all its anger, "The Lie" is really quite religious. It is his soul that survives after all the falsehoods are exposed. On the verge of losing everything, Ralegh seemed to reconsider what was worth having. It is almost as if he wanted to be stripped down so that he could hold fast to something deeper and truer than his bows, smiles, gifts, and schemes.

Faced with total destruction, Ralegh seemed to blame himself for having hoped to rise, rather than Elizabeth for threatening to bring him down. In another poem, his "Farewell to the Court," he lamented his "truthless dreams." His own "dreams" were the lies. The glittering "joys" of the court to which he devoted his life were mere illusions. In a line that seemed to reverse his entire career of ambition and struggle, he wrote, "Desire attained is not desire, / But as the cinders to the fire."

Ralegh played the royal love game, believing he could win. But when he lost, he realized he had been fooling himself all along. Beneath his anger was resignation.

These poems help explain one of the great mysteries of Ralegh's fall. If he had been merely ambitious, all he needed to do was spurn or pay off the pregnant lady. That was a quick way to reconcile with the queen. Instead, he chose to marry his own Elizabeth, which was the worst betrayal of all. Perhaps after one too many days of flattering the aging queen, fighting the churn of envy as Essex replaced him by her side, and scrambling to hide another dalliance with a pretty maid, Ralegh wanted the play to end. He may have chosen the simple human love of a woman who could be a wife and mother, even at the cost of the boundless love of a queen who was part person, part goddess, and part England itself.

ALL THE WORLD'S A STAGE

Ralegh was both a brilliantly convincing suitor and an unsparing critic of the masks at court, but he was not a mere hypocrite. While he plotted, calculated, wrote love poetry, and worshiped Elizabeth, another voice in his mind said this was all a play and at any moment the curtain might come crashing down. Realizing that they were playing many roles forced Ralegh and his contemporaries to try to figure out what endured after all the changes. This was the great problem of their age.

One of Shakespeare's most famous speeches describes just this issue:

> *All the world's a stage,*
> *And all the men and women merely players:*
> *They have their exits and their entrances;*
> *And one man in his time plays many parts,*
> *His acts being seven ages.*

The seven ages of man is an ancient idea, and Shakespeare is telling us to live as is appropriate for our time of life. Read that way, he is saying precisely, "Act your age." But the idea of acting also introduces the opposite meaning. If we "play many parts," that may not just be in growing older. It can mean that we pretend to be many different people. We can become what we need to be.

All over the world Protestants and Catholics were at war over religion. New discoveries in science were pushing the earth out of its place at the center of universe. Explorations and conquests kept challenging old beliefs about the world. People wanted certainty but could not trust that anything would remain stable from day to day. One answer was to lie, to give a false face to the changing world while you pursued your own ends. The clearest statement of this view was Niccolò Machiavelli's *The Prince*, published in 1532. It argued that lies were necessary in politics, and therefore even good. The ends, Machiavelli claimed, justify the means. This was such a stark, cold defense of manipulation that to be Machiavellian came to mean being unscrupulous. But Machiavelli merely put down on paper what everyone already practiced. And yet people still yearned for some truth beyond the shuffling of many masks. Acting all the time and knowing that you are doing it can be both painful and sobering. It makes for great literature.

In Shakespeare's plays characters have soliloquies—monologues in which they reveal their inner thoughts. The word for that kind of speech did not even exist before his day. Confused by all the conflicting parts they played to please others, Elizabethans were forced to speak for themselves, as individuals. The most famous soliloquy of all is Hamlet's wrestling with "to be or not to be." Sounding very much like a cross between Ralegh's poems "Ocean to Cynthia" and "The Lie," it is a moment when a person sees how false the world is, verges on suicide, and stops only for fear of "what dreams may come" in the afterlife. To the Elizabethans life was a play, and balancing between heaven and earth, the players constantly struggled to figure out their parts. Ralegh's smiling flattery and his fierce contempt for lies made him a perfect representative of his age—the time of both Machiavelli and Shakespeare. He was a great calculator, and an eloquent recorder of the cost of living a double life.

Ralegh acted out another kind of double role while he was imprisoned in his home. Durham House faced the Thames River. Hearing that the queen was to land nearby, he flew into a fury, claiming she had been sent there to torture him. According to a report, he pleaded to be able to row out "to ease his mind but with a sight of the queen; or else, he protested, his heart would break." When the jailer refused, Ralegh appeared to attack him. We know it was all a show because Ralegh attached a note to this report on a small slip of paper that could easily be removed. It read, "If you let the Queen's Majesty know hereof, as you think good." He was playing the part of the love-mad suitor, the prisoner of passion driven to crazed combat by the prospect of seeing his beloved. Although his wild emotions were contrived, regaining the queen's love was his only hope. Mad to be free, he played a man driven mad by love.

THE MOTHER OF PRIZES

Soon after this display of theatrical passion the royal prisoner and his bride were moved to the dread Tower of London. While his dramatic acts of courtly love produced no effect, another of his lifetime interests did. Long before the queen discovered his marriage, he had sent ships out to take Spanish prizes. They succeeded beyond anyone's dreams, capturing what was said to be the largest ship in the world. The Portuguese carrack *Madre de Dios* was groaning under the weight of the precious cargo it carried: some 537 tons of spices, as well as pearls, silks, ivory, silver, and gold. The royal treasurer estimated the value of the prize at half a million pounds. But the booty was disappearing rapidly.

Spices were valuable, small, transportable, and very easy to steal. Once the boat put into port in Dartmouth, the lucrative and fragrant mounds of cloves, peppercorns, cinnamon, mace, and nutmeg proved irresistible to anyone who could get near them. Many important people, including the queen herself, had invested in this bit of privateering, and they were seeing their profits whisked off into hundreds of untraceable hands. Only one man possessed the good faith of the people of Devon and the authority to stop the thefts. But he was in prison. Ralegh was set free on a short leash and given the task of recovering the stolen spices so that his jailers could make back their investment.

Ralegh did his job well, but that hardly soothed the queen. When she divided up the spoils, he received a distinctly miserly portion, not even enough to cover his investment in sending ships out to sea. "I took all the care and pains," he complained, while some who risked nothing "have double." Still, there were other kinds of rewards. Elizabeth had put eighteen hundred pounds, a relatively small amount, into the adventure. She awarded herself eighty thousand pounds out of the jackpot. That was, Ralegh knew, "more than ever a man presented Her Majesty." He hoped that "if God have sent it for my ransom . . . Her Majesty . . . will accept it." She did and she didn't. She chose not to punish him in the way he feared and his enemies hoped—by taking away his offices and licenses. And by the end of 1592 she allowed the Raleghs to leave the Tower and move to their country home at Sherborne. But she did not forgive him. His betrayal had cut too deep for that. Instead she maintained her silence and waited.

BEYOND THE HORIZON

When he returned to Parliament, a humbled Ralegh who was no longer part of the royal court showed that he could understand how hard it was to be an outsider. He suggested taking the poorest people off the tax rolls and, instead, increasing the tax on those who could afford it. When a bill came up that would have been extremely harsh to Catholics, even taking their children away to be raised under the eye of the government, he stood against it. He opposed any bill in which "men's intentions shall be judged by a jury." This tolerant view was not only highly unusual for the time but a total change from the grim religious battles he had fought in France and Ireland.

When he was alone with his friends, clear thinkers such as Hariot, Dee, and Marlowe, Ralegh's own views of religion crossed from toleration into skepticism. In a time when the astronomical theories of Copernicus were considered close to heretical, and curiosity about the New World was associated with disbelief in biblical creation, such open-mindedness was highly suspect.

And then, one fine evening in 1593, Ralegh went to dinner with a group of friends and family and a local vicar named Ralph Ironside. In the high-spirited banter the educated but not terribly bright Ironside was challenged about his beliefs: "Soul, what is that?" This set off a round of debate over the fundamentals of religion. The vicar kept resorting to abstract Latin definitions, while Ralegh and his crew pushed for clarity and logic, though much of this was wordplay.

What must have seemed a diverting match of wits to men who enjoyed puzzling out the mysteries of the New World was more disturbing to the vicar, and in 1594 a charge of atheism was laid against Ralegh at the Court of High Commission. Nothing came of this allegation, in part because some of the judges were old Devon friends and one had even been part of the dinnertime debate. Still, it reflected what many people thought of Sir Walter. Shakespeare's *Love's Labour's Lost*, a play about a strange academy, may be a barbed satire directed at Ralegh and the freethinking men around him.

Ralegh was not an atheist, but he set no limits on where his mind could probe. He was willing to consider any idea before finally deciding what he believed. When he was by Elizabeth's side, he used that clarity to entertain and advise her. Now that he was in disgrace, he let his mind roam further. For the first time in nearly twenty years he could travel as far as his dreams could take him.

In 1586 Ralegh's agents had captured a Spanish gentleman named Don Sarmiento de Gamboa. A soldier in the campaign against Tupac Amaru, the last Inca, he later chronicled the entire conquest of Peru. Ralegh treated his enemy well and used his charm to get him to talk. The noble don finally revealed one of the great secrets of the Spanish empire. The lost gold of the Incas was now housed in the missing kingdom of El Dorado. This was astonishing; but was it true, or was Sarmiento playing a double game with his captor?

In 1594 a captain named George Popham seized new Spanish documents that contained an eyewitness tale that matched Sarmiento's story. The evidence was adding up, one set of secret sources corroborating the others. This was too much for Ralegh to resist.

As long as Ralegh was one of Elizabeth's favorites, she made sure he never sailed too far from her side. He was too valuable to risk overseas. Now that he was married to another woman, the queen cut that emotional cord. She no longer cared to stop him from going off on dangerous and mad adventures.

This was the paradox of his disgrace. He was out of favor with the queen, which meant he was finally free to devote himself to his lifetime quest. He could leave because of her anger, and yet leaving gave him a way to regain her favor. Only an overseas kingdom could win back the queen or, if she should prove unrelenting, support him financially. Ireland was not working out. Virginia had failed. There was yet one more hope across the horizon, and it was the most dazzling of all. In 1595, half sailing away from the queen's ominous silence, half sailing toward a dream, Sir Walter Ralegh set off to win the lost empire of El Dorado.

Chapter 11

THE DISCOVERY
OF THE GOLDEN KINGDOM

This is the story Ralegh pieced together from Sarmiento's story and Popham's documents.

A bronzed Spaniard had stumbled out of the jungle carrying two gourds filled with golden beads. Juan Martín de Albujar had been there, to the great city of Manoa, capital of El Dorado. Albujar was in charge of guns and gunpowder for an expedition that failed when the powder exploded. As punishment he was marooned on a raft and set adrift to die. But he was rescued and taken blindfolded on a difficult journey. After fourteen days he reached Great Manoa and was allowed to look around. Ralegh recorded that "he traveled all that day through the city, and the next day from sun rising to sun setting, ere he came to the palace of the Inca."

Manoa was more than the center of a hidden kingdom of vast wealth. It harbored the greatest treasure in all the world: the vast reserves of gold the

Incas had managed to hide from the Spanish. Once a year, in this city that fairly shone with gold, there was a special ceremony: A fine spray of gold powder was blown on the body of the king, El Dorado.

Albujar was allowed to leave, taking proof of what he had witnessed. But once he left the safety of the region controlled by these wealthy and civilized people, he was robbed and left to scramble back to the coast with his gourds. Though Albujar was dead and his precious beads were missing, the way to El Dorado was now clear. It was on Lake Manoa in the Guiana highlands, between the Amazon and the Orinoco rivers. Somewhere through the tangle of jungle, across the seas of grass, amid the weird rock outcroppings that thrust up from the savanna like relics of a prehistoric age, lay the golden land of the golden man.

The story of Albujar's journey sent Ralegh across the ocean. When he landed on Trinidad in April of 1595, he stumbled across the perfect confirmation of all he had heard. On this island, which sits just off the coast of South America, Ralegh found and imprisoned the aged Spaniard who knew more about El Dorado than anyone else, Don Antonio de Berrío.

Gonzalo Jiménez de Quesada, that intrepid seeker after El Dorado whom we met in the prologue as one of the last great conquistadors, had died in 1579. He named his niece as the heir to his claim on the golden kingdom, under one very demanding condition. Her husband would have to devote himself to continuing the quest. Berrío, a soldier already in his fifties, was that man. In 1581 he sailed off to America with his wife and three children to fulfill his destiny. By the time Ralegh captured him fourteen years later, in 1595, Berrío had made three horrifyingly difficult trips into the interior, following one rumor after another. During the last one he imitated Cortés, killing all his men's horses so that the men could never turn back but only plow farther on into hostile lands. Now in his mid-seventies, Berrío was in Trinidad to gather his forces for yet one more backbreaking expedition.

Berrío was proof positive. He was the direct link to the age of conquistadors, the living heir to the Spanish frenzy to find El Dorado. Since he was in Trinidad, the golden kingdom could not be far away. Ralegh now knew exactly where it must be. As he recorded it in the book he wrote when he returned to England, "The Empire of Guiana is directly east from Peru towards the sea . . . and it hath more abundance of gold than any part of Peru." The Incas must have fled due east and settled in a place directly on the equator. Ralegh assumed a sunny place like that would be most likely to have gold, the sun's metal.

When Ralegh captured Berrío and revealed his determination to find El Dorado, the old Spaniard "was stricken into a great melancholy and sadness." How gratifying. The more upset Berrío seemed, the more sure Ralegh could be that the golden city was nearby. But Berrío did not just sulk, and that complicated the picture. Instead, he insisted that the trip was not worth making, for the crew would "suffer many miseries" once they entered the jungle. Berrío protested that the rivers were too shallow to sail and insisted that the natives would provide neither information nor food nor gold. Ralegh assumed that Berrío was trying to discourage him to keep the prize for himself. But in his book he admitted that most of the warnings later came true.

Ralegh and the Spaniard were chasing the same dream. For that very reason each saw in the other's interest proof that the myths and stories were true. But were they learning from each other or confirming each other's delusions? There was no way to know but by entering the jungle. Even then, how could Ralegh judge the new land but by the knowledge of the old? His

The capture of Antonio de Berrío, from a later edition of Ralegh's report in De Bry's America.

book *The Discoverie of the Large, Rich and Bewtiful Empyre of Guiana* tells us more about his own beliefs than it does of the slow, black rivers that feed into the Orinoco Delta, or of the fishermen and warriors who lived alongside them.

Ralegh's first challenge was to find his way into the continent.

I know all the earth doth not yield the like confluence of streams and branches, the one crossing the other so many times, and all so fair and large, and so like one to another, as no man can tell which to take: and if we went by the Sun or compass hoping thereby to go directly one way or other, yet that way we also carried in a circle amongst multitudes of islands, and every island so bordered with high trees, as no man could see any further than the breadth of the river.

But in time they came upon a real river. Ralegh named it the Red Cross, perhaps after the red Cross of Saint George that appears on the English flag.

Soon the party spotted a canoe carrying three men. The English overtook the craft but did not attack it. Seeing this, watchers on the shore came forward, ready to trade and talk. From the start, Ralegh wanted to show the natives that the English would treat them better than did the Spaniards. When he met native caciques (chiefs) in Trinidad, he "made them understand that I was a servant of a Queen, who was a great cacique of the north, and a virgin, and had more cacique under her than there were trees in their island; that she was an enemy of the Castellani [Spanish] in respect of their tyranny and oppression." Ralegh thought that it was American gold that allowed Spain to be such a dangerous global power. If he could make an alliance with native Americans, while also finding a source of gold rivaling that already controlled by the Spaniards, he would totally change the balance of power all around the world.

Throughout the journey Ralegh made sure his men behaved honorably toward the natives, and especially in a way that we do not usually associate with European conquest. He insisted that not one person could "take from

MARGARITA

CARIBBEAN SEA

Ralegh attacks, 1595

Fort
San
Josef

TRINIDAD

Serpent's Mouth

GUIANA

San Thomé
Ralegh sets anchor, 1595

English attack,
1618

Orinoco R.

Ralegh
explores,
1595

Caroni R.

El Callao,
site of gold mine
exploited in
later centuries

Scale of 100 miles

Where El Dorado
was thought to lie

*Guiana
Highlands*

RALEGH'S
QUEST

KL

any of the natives so much as a pina [pineapple], or a potato root, without giving them contentment [paying them]." Even more important, no man could make any advances at all toward their beautiful "wives or daughters." He hoped this would distinguish his men from "the Spaniards (who tyrannize over them in all things)" and make the natives "admire her Majesty, whose commandment I told them it was."

Ralegh knew his virgin queen all too well. She would not be pleased at reports of English sexual adventure. In one way this was a strategy of empire building. If the impulsive Spanish forced themselves on native women, the English could win native allies by their respectful restraint. But it was also good domestic politics. Alliances made in the queen's name would have to be chaste.

Ralegh crossed an ocean to conquer an empire. And yet his account does not sound like the triumph of superior Europeans over American inferiors. After the bargaining at the riverbank, a local chief trapped one of Ralegh's men and killed him. Ralegh's response was merely to take as captive an old man who could serve as guide. Ralegh thought these natives were "a very goodly people and very valiant, and have the most manly speech and most deliberate that ever I heard." Not only were they well-spoken, they were good-looking: "In all my life, either in the Indies, or in Europe, did I never behold a more goodly or better favored people."

The next leg of the trip was trying. Though they finally reached a straight and swift river, what is now called the Manamo, they were rowing against the current. The only way he could get his men to push on hour after hour, day after day, in the extreme heat and humidity, against the force of the river, was to keep telling the pilots to "promise an end the next day." They did this again and again, pretending that food, water, and rest were just four "reaches" ahead, then three, then two, then one. All this was pure invention—or motivation, if you prefer. As the men grew weaker and weaker, "we were brought into despair and discomfort." Only a final lie— the promise that their goal lay a single day ahead—and a final threat—that the "world would also laugh us to scorn" if they gave up so quickly—kept the men rowing.

The one consolation in this difficult stretch was the beauty and bounty of nature. They saw "birds of all colors, some carnation, some crimson, orange tawny, purple, green . . . and of all other sorts both simple and mixed, and it was unto us a great good passing of the time to behold them, besides the relief we found by killing some store of them." However difficult their journey, nature was an ally, not an enemy.

The next day, when the captive native offered to lead a smaller group to food and drink, Ralegh agreed. But as hour after hour passed, the guide echoed Ralegh's own promises, claiming the place was just "a little farther." This kept up all day, until toward night he said it was still a way ahead.

Suspecting that this was all a trick, and that the guide might be an agent of the Spanish, the English threatened to kill him. And they would have, too, if they had known the way back to the rest of their men. But it was now "dark as pitch, and the river began so to narrow itself, and the trees to hang over from side to side," that they had to hack through the overhanging branches with swords. The English had eaten only a light breakfast, assuming they were a short trip from a real feast. Now they were lost on a black river in the black night, forty miles from their companions, and starving. Finally, at one in the morning, just as their suspicions of the pilot reached a peak, they saw a light ahead. This was a village of the Arawak people, a true haven.

The natives were friendly and willing to trade. The English left with food and even *cachire,* an alcohol women make by chewing palm plants and then spitting out the liquid. Their saliva helps it to ferment. Many people, from Ralegh's day to the present, have reported that it is a pleasing drink.

The following day, calm and refreshed, Ralegh came upon one of the great moments of the trip. As he rowed down the river back to the main boat, he

passed the most beautiful country that ever mine eyes beheld, and whereas all that we had seen before was nothing but woods, prickles, bushes and thorns, here we beheld plains of twenty miles in length, the grass short and green, and in divers parts groves of trees by themselves, as if they had been by all the art and labor in the world so made of purpose. And still as we rowed, the deer came down feeding by the water's side, as if they had been used to a keeper's call.

Here was the real golden land. After the dark night of fear, after fighting the jungle and the current, he had come to a kind of beauty that took his breath away. Not the rainbow of wild-bird colors. No, here nature had an order of its own. The grass seemed cut, the trees carefully spaced. Even the deer, that royal animal kept in deer parks in England, were peaceful and well trained.

Ralegh was not exaggerating. If you travel along a river to the Orinoco plains, you will see exactly this kind of scene. The land really does seem to be managed by nature itself. Yet there must have been something in Ralegh that could appreciate this natural Eden. A land untouched by Europeans did not need to be tamed. Instead, it seemed well managed by a divine designer.

Just after describing the deer, Ralegh added a twist, which only made his

The banks of the Orinoco today. It is easy to see why Ralegh thought it seemed to be a kind of natural garden under divine management. (COURTESY MARICEL PRESILLA)

story more biblical: "Upon this river there were great store of fowl, and of many sorts. We saw in it divers sorts of strange fishes, & of a marvellous bigness, but for lagartos [alligators] it exceeded, for there were thousands of those ugly serpents." In Eden there was an evil snake. Just as Ralegh arrived at the place that was most like that perfect garden, he saw thousands of ugly, serpentine alligators. He even lost one crew member, a "very proper young Negro" who jumped in to swim and was "devoured." Real or invented, this transplanted African made Ralegh's story all the more universal, and his death was a reminder of the fate all humans have shared since we left the last perfect garden.

If Ralegh had ended his journey here, it would have been an argument to leave America alone. Once you find Eden, what can you do but protect it? But the very next event reminds us that his mission had just the opposite aim. Ralegh and his lead group rejoined their mates and shared the Arawak food. Then another small party set off to look for the next landing. On the way they saw four canoes speeding away like startled animals. Everyone gave chase, and the party soon stumbled into a very exciting clue. First they found two of the canoes. "Nothing on the earth could have been more welcome to us next unto gold, than the great store of very excellent bread which we found in those canoes."

Then, as he was "creeping through the bushes," Ralegh "saw an Indian basket, hidden." In it were a Spanish refiner's tools. One of the men who had just fled past on the river was a Spaniard who had been up ahead, testing rocks for gold. Ralegh was thrilled. His enemies, the people who knew most about the location of El Dorado, were on exactly the same track as he was. Both the fabled lost kingdom and the mines that gave it its wealth must be nearby. "Defended with rocks of hard stone, which we call the white spar," was the very best gold ore. In one breath Ralegh gave a vision of an unspoiled American Eden; in the next he showed how much gold meant to him, and he looked forward to smashing rocks apart to find it.

The next day their good fortune continued when an important cacique named Toparimaca arrived with thirty or forty followers. The two leaders treated each other well, the chieftain offering local fruits, bread, fish, meat, and *cachire,* and the Englishman reciprocating with Spanish wine. After eating, Ralegh went to visit Toparimaca's village and saw two caciques lolling in hammocks, "& two women attending them with six cups and little ladles to fill them, out of an earthen pitcher of wine, and so they drank each of them three of those cups at a time."

A later engraving of the scene in which Ralegh lost a crew member to a serpent just as they reached an Edenic spot.

With Toparimaca's brother as guide, the English sailed up the river. There was a sense of calm in this stretch of the journey. Ralegh's captains had time to investigate and admire the surrounding countryside. Around June 9, twenty-three days into the journey, Ralegh's men reached the village of Morequito. Here they could meet one of the most important caciques, the ancient Topiawari. Perhaps he was not really 110 years old, as Ralegh claimed, but he was clearly a respected and powerful man.

Ralegh treated Topiawari as both a potential ally and a good source of information on Manoa. He heard exactly what he wanted to hear. The old man told him that when he was a young man,

> there came down into that large valley of Guiana, a nation from so far off as the Sun slept (for such were his own words) with so great a multitude as they could not be numbered nor resisted, & and that they wore large coats, and hats of crimson color, which color he expressed, by showing a piece of red wood . . . those that had slain and rooted out so many of the ancient people as there were leaves in the wood upon all the trees, and had now made themselves Lords of all . . . built a great town . . . and that their houses have many rooms, one over the other, and that therein the great king . . . kept three thousand men to defend the borders against them.

Here it was, direct proof, straight from the mouth of an ancient lord. In his lifetime the fleeing Incas had arrived, defeated his own people, and established their powerful kingdom. No one could expect Ralegh to go much further. His small band had no chance against such a large army. But he now had just the information needed to return with a real force, if Topiawari's account was to be believed.

Ralegh hears the story of El Dorado *from Topiawari, as reconstructed in De Bry's* America.

Ralegh reported this conversation so carefully that it reads like a novel. He made sure to point out that the chief defined the red color by pointing to wood and counted people by leaves on the trees. Perhaps he scripted a native-sounding speech for this ancient lord so that he could persuade his own queen to send an army to the Orinoco.

But there may have been a different game going on as well. By the time Ralegh reached this region, the natives already had a lot of experience dealing with Europeans sailing up their river, searching for El Dorado. Topiawari might have been telling Ralegh a story just to keep the Englishman moving on up ahead, out of the way of his people. We will never know whether Ralegh really heard something similar to Topiawari's speech and added to it, whether the old man was deceiving him, or whether Ralegh invented it entirely.

The next day Ralegh reached the confluence of the Orinoco and the Caroni. There he heard more versions of tales similar to Topiawari's, as well as rumors of a large silver mine. Gazing out across the plains, he saw some

> ten or twelve overfalls [waterfalls] . . . every one as high over the other as a church tower, which fell with that fury, that the rebound of waters made it seem, as if it had been all covered over with a great shower of rain: and in some places we took it at the first for a smoke that had risen over some great town.

After describing this stunning landscape—which can actually be found on the Caroni, though not exactly where he put it—Ralegh concluded his trip up the Orinoco with a kind of travel agent's advertisement:

> I never saw a more beautiful country, nor more lively prospects, hills so raised here and there over the valleys, the river winding into divers branches, the plains adjoining without bush or stubble, all fair green grass . . . the air fresh with a gentle easterly wind, and every stone that we stooped to take up, promised either gold or silver by his complexion.

Shortly after seeing this, Ralegh's crew turned their barges back and began the difficult trip that took them through the storm to the Serpent's Mouth and then back to England.

What, then, was the gold of El Dorado? Was it the treasure city that

This map is the result of Ralegh's journey. At the center, under the word Guiana, is the supposed Lake Paria, and just after the letter "A" is the golden city of Manoa. Toward the bottom are the headless men and Amazon warriors that also appear in his report. The map added both solid information and pure legend to the Europeans' store of knowledge about America.

(COURTESY THE BRITISH LIBRARY)

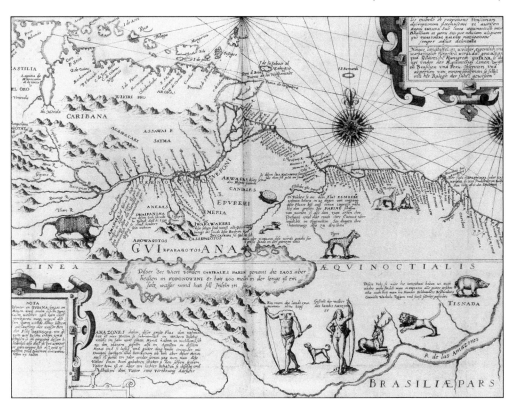

Topiawari confirmed lay just a few days' march ahead in the highlands? Easy pickings, perhaps, for a large-enough English force. Was it the ore that seemed to be strewn everywhere about? The fleeing Spaniard who hid his refiner's tools suggested that these mines had better be nabbed before the enemy got them. Was it the strong people with their attractive women? Or was it the stunningly beautiful land, which seemed so ready to farm that it almost managed itself?

As Ralegh ended his report, he looked back at all these golden dreams and summed up what this place meant to him.

> Guiana is a country that hath yet her maidenhead, never sacked, turned, nor wrought. The face of the earth has not yet been torn, nor the virtue and salt of the soil spent by manurance. The graves have not been opened for gold, the mines not broken open with sledges, nor their images pulled down out of their temples. It hath never been entered by any army of strength, and never conquered or possessed by any Christian prince.

This passage is the best description we have of what the New World meant to the Europeans. In one way it is an invitation to the English to rush over and take everything they can get their hands on—ore, land, statues. Guiana is a helpless virgin, it says; come violate her. And yet its main meaning is just the opposite. Guiana is a truly virgin land. Leave it alone. The country as a whole is just like all those beautiful women Ralegh protected. Once Christians come, they will "sack," "rend," and "tear" it, they will ruin the "virtue" of its soil with fertilizer, and "pull down" its sacred images.

These words are the true gold of Ralegh's quest for El Dorado. They show how irresistible the treasure of the new lands was to a strong and determined person like Ralegh. Yet they reveal that at least one such exceptional man knew he could only destroy what he was so desperate to possess. The discovery in his book is not of the large, rich, and beautiful empire of Guiana, but of the clash in Ralegh's large, deep, and conflicted heart.

Chapter 12

MY LORD OF ESSEX

Ralegh's life was a series of romantic adventures. He starred in one epic after another, each complete with swashbuckling swordplay, sweet poetry, wide-screen heroes and villains. In the long sweep of his life, though, some of the best scenes turned out to have subplots that changed their meaning entirely, from grand triumph to sad decline.

When he returned from South America full of tales of golden kingdoms, rich mines, and visions of Eden, few believed him. Skeptics claimed he had been hiding out in Cornwall all along and that his precious ore samples were not even from the New World. Ralegh wrote his *Discoverie* to prove his claims, and his words were more persuasive than his deeds. The book quickly became an international success, with many editions all over Europe. Writers from Shakespeare to John Donne, and later John Milton, eagerly used it as a source for their own work. But Elizabeth did not respond. She showed no interest in spending money on New World ventures, or even in forgiving the suitor who tried to find paradise to regain her favor.

Since Ralegh was unable to seduce the queen with promises of new kingdoms, his best chance to prove himself was in fighting Spain. There again his very greatest successes had dark undertones.

Take Cádiz. In mid-June of 1596 the English fleet was bobbing off the coast of this wealthiest city in Spain. The Earl of Essex, the queen's favorite, was one of the commanders. As Ralegh fell from favor and struggled to win his way back, Essex soared. He was the queen's late love, half naughty child, half bold suitor.

Cádiz was Essex's stage to prove his mettle, to show that a new generation of leaders could take the mantle from the giants of the Armada. "I know God hath a great work to work by me," he wrote an ally. "I will make all the world see I understand myself."

Essex's sense of destiny came as much from the fading of old leaders as it did from his own confidence. In the previous months, just as Ralegh published his account of his search for El Dorado, two of England's titans had died following their own New World dreams. Sir Francis Drake and Sir John Hawkins were England's two best sea captains. From their raids and battles in the Caribbean to the heroic days of the Armada, they had constantly outthought, outfought, and outwilled the Spanish all around the globe. (This great soldiering did not necessarily make them great men. Their sea adventures began when they initiated and defended the practice of buying slaves in Africa and taking them to the Americas.) Yet they both died of disease in an inglorious failed effort to revisit the Caribbean once again. With them also died their style of war: a cross between piracy for profit and brilliant individual blows against Spain.

Although the defeat of the Armada bought time for England, it did not end the Spanish threat. Philip II was as determined as ever to destroy the Protestant queen. In 1595 soldiers on four Spanish ships had sailed across the channel, burned three Cornish villages, and said Mass on English soil. While this caused little real damage, it showed how vulnerable the island nation remained. Ralegh kept getting intelligence reports that Philip was gathering another large fleet for a final assault on England. Since Drake was gone and could not lead another attack on Cádiz, as he'd done so marvelously in 1587, other captains would have to take his place. A direct attack on Cádiz would prevent Spain from invading England for at least one more year.

While Essex was the most dynamic figure in the English fleet off Cádiz, its real leader was the aging Lord Admiral Charles Howard, who had commanded the fleet against the Armada. Howard and Essex did not get along. By 1596 Howard knew that "my time will be past after this for doing any more." But he was absolutely unwilling to let a new generation take charge. When he saw Essex's name next to his on a report to the queen, he grabbed a knife and cut it out. He "would have none so high as himself." No over-reaching young lord was going to be his equal. Everyone could sense the danger of this growing clash between the old leaders and the new. "I see already," one young observer wrote, "the fire kindled that must consume us."

The invasion fleet was most impressive: ninety-six English ships with six thousand soldiers and five thousand marines eager for the chance to go on a plundering spree. Then there were the twenty-four ships carrying the Dutch, bent on vengeance against their Spanish masters. They were joined by perhaps a thousand gentlemen decked out in feathers, gold, and silver lace. This large force of ships and soldiers was again split into four squadrons, each of which had a distinctive flag on its lead ship. Essex flew his familiar tawny orange, Admiral Howard displayed crimson, his nephew Lord Thomas Howard favored blue, while on Ralegh's *Warspite* white flapped in the breeze. Though Ralegh was in disfavor, he was respected as a fighter and as a devoted enemy of the Spanish.

Spanish lookouts first spied the far-off sails of the British navy on June 15. June 20 fell on a Sunday. That morning the bells of Cádiz rang out, but not for Mass. Instead, they were clanging a warning that the enemy had arrived. Luck favored the English. There were only four galleons in the harbor to oppose them. And waiting at anchor were nearly forty heavily laden merchant ships about to sail to America. This rich fleet was filled with valuable goods needed to reprovision the Spanish colonies.

The English were thrilled. "What a sudden rejoicing there was!" exclaimed the lord admiral's doctor. "How every man skipped and leapt for joy." Victory and wealth were there for the taking. Ralegh must have felt something even stronger and darker. The four Spanish galleons were the *St. Philip*, the *St. Andrew*, the *St. Matthew*, and the *St. Thomas*, nicknamed the Four Apostles. Five years earlier the first two had been part of a fleet of fifty-three Spanish ships that had surprised six English ships off the Azores. While most of the English had escaped, one captain, Ralegh's cousin Sir Richard Grenville, had made a different choice. Whether out of mad pride or to hold off the enemy so the others could retreat, he sailed the *Revenge* directly into murderous fire. As Ralegh put it, "Sir Richard utterly refused to turn from the enemy, alleging that he would rather choose to die than to dishonor himself, his country, and her Majesty's ship."

Grenville fought so desperately and with such valor that the Spanish offered him extremely lenient terms of surrender. He refused, insisting that the *Revenge* be sunk so that the Spanish could never claim to have taken an English ship. When his few remaining men begged not to drown, Grenville finally agreed to be taken captive. But he would give the Spanish no satisfaction. When they offered him a drink, he smashed the glass and ate the shards, preferring his own English blood to their sweet wine. He died soon after.

Hearing of Grenville's fate, Ralegh quickly wrote a short, intense "report" on the battle. That vivid account defined British heroism and courage for generations of readers. Sitting in the *Warspite* just outside Cádiz harbor, Ralegh had a more immediate use for his vengeful feelings. He "resolved to be revenged for the *Revenge,* or to second her with mine own life."

Poised to destroy an enemy he hated with a very personal passion, Ralegh had to wait. Essex and Howard could not decide how to attack. Which should they hit first: the city with its forts and guns, the four well-armed galleons, or the rich merchant ships? They wasted most of the day talking, and then Essex attempted a confused and late assault on the city. The wind made landing even more difficult, but Essex was determined to try again—and the English were on their way to bungling their golden opportunity.

Ralegh put an end to that. At six in the morning of June 21 he sailed up to Essex's ship, the *Due Repulse*, boarded it, and demanded that the impetuous lord change plans. Somehow Essex managed to listen to a man who was both his subordinate and his rival, only protesting that he was acting on Howard's orders. Ralegh was not daunted. He rushed over to the flagship of the greatest naval commander in all England and argued so passionately and clearly that he changed even the lord admiral's mind. Instead of Essex's solo landing against big guns, they would first take out the galleons, then pour into the undefended harbor.

Exhilarated, Ralegh dashed back to the *Due Repulse* and yelled out to Essex, *"Entramos, entramos"*—"We're going in, we're going in." As his men cheered wildly, Essex tossed his plumed hat in the air. Ralegh's iron will had overcome the divisions between the commanders. After that, crushing the Spanish would be easy. By the time Ralegh convinced both leaders, it was noon. It took the rest of the day to organize everyone to execute his plan. A day had been lost and a battle won.

On June 22 each English squadron was assigned to take out one of the

The English navy approaching Cádiz. The Four Apostles' cannons are blazing, but they soon fell.

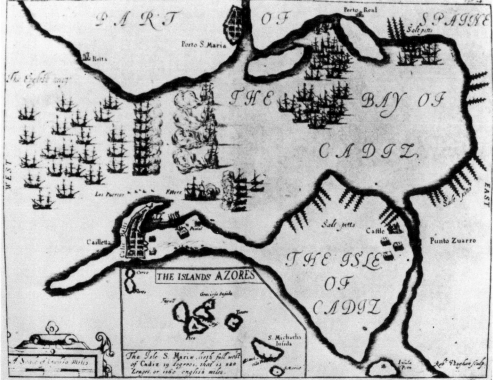

apostles. Out of respect for Ralegh, he was given the challenge he wanted— the *St. Philip*, the biggest and deadliest ship, the very one that had sent Grenville to his death.

Ralegh sailed into battle with the same wild confidence he showed in challenging Essex and Howard. As the *Warspite* neared the galleon, the harbor guns fired, loud but ineffective. Ralegh calmly lined his trumpeters on deck and gave an answer, mocking the weak Spanish cannon with sour horn blasts. But the Spaniards were only half of his problem.

Now that the fighting was about to start, with real honor and spoils at stake, each English captain was out for himself. Racing to the *St. Philip*, Ralegh found that another English ship had locked onto his with a grappling iron. He sliced it off. With some daring and clever sailing the *Warspite* reached its goal. Seeing the English about to overwhelm them, the Spanish tried to flee and ran themselves aground. Two of the four galleons burst into flames before they could be captured. The other two were not so lucky. Dying men were trapped between flames and English guns, "very many hanging by the ropes' ends by the ships' sides, under the water even to the lips; many swimming with grievous wounds." Even Ralegh felt that "if any man had a desire to see Hell itself, it was there."

There were two kinds of hell in the fighting. The inferno of burning sails and drowning men was one. Though not one English sailor died, the victory was not without cost. In the midst of the fighting a cannonball hit the deck next to Ralegh, and the splinters exploded into his leg. As a result, he could not take part in the plunder, and for the rest of his life he walked with a limp. The second hell was the continual infighting and competition among the English. If Protestant individualism made it easier for Elizabeth's men to defeat Spain's great Armada, it also made it nearly impossible for them to cooperate with one another in large expeditions. Rather than being a total victory for the English, Cádiz was a warning of the treachery, pride, and murderous power struggles to come.

After destroying the Apostles, Ralegh sent delegates to the other commanders to agree on an acceptable ransom for the immensely valuable cargo of the now-helpless merchant fleet. According to one source, it was worth approximately ten times the English Crown's average annual income. The soldiers were too busy with the spoils of the city to answer. The Spanish offered two million ducats, a quarter of what Ralegh expected. The English leadership again broke into squabbling factions debating over huge sums. And then the issue was decided for them. The Spanish commander decided that denying the English their plunder was worth more than any cargo, and he burned the entire fleet.

Cádiz was a triumph for Ralegh. His bravery won the queen, and by June of 1597 he regained his honored position as captain of her guard. It was an even greater success for Essex, who was seen as the handsome hero who had destroyed the Spanish. "Spain," one account read, "never received so great an overthrow, so great a spoil, so great an indignity at our hands as in that journey to Cadiz." And yet the entire campaign really showed how factional and divided the English had become. Luck gave them a great chance, which they nearly wasted. The commanders' vast fleet left Spain with only a fraction of the wealth they should have brought back. However pleased Elizabeth may have been with her dashing courtiers, she was angry at their failure to capture or at least ransom the merchant fleet. Between the queen's displeasure and the rifts that the conflict exposed, Cádiz was as much a sign of the ending of Elizabeth's golden age as it was a highlight of her reign.

Chapter 13

MISCHIEVOUS MATCHIVEL

By the turn of the century Elizabeth had lived longer than any English monarch in memory. This posed a special challenge to her court. The problem was no longer just to win the favor of a queen increasingly dependent on wigs and powders to hide her age, but to do that while also courting whoever would follow. This double game doomed the heroes of Cádiz.

As a virgin queen Elizabeth could have no direct heirs. Who, then, should succeed her? King James VI of Scotland, who was descended from her grandfather Henry VII, was the most plausible choice. Plausible does not mean certain, and Elizabeth kept delaying her decision, which left ever more room for maneuvering and alliances. At the same time, James entertained plots to overthrow her and install himself in her place. Sitting across the border in Scotland, he kept testing out which of England's lords would support him when his great moment came.

Essex was the ill-fitting piece in this intricate puzzle of succession. He was so popular with both the queen and the fighting men that he might upset anyone's calculations and even become king himself. Essex's exceptionally clear-sighted adviser, Francis Bacon, realized that everything that gave the earl hope also placed him in danger. He saw that "a man of a nature not to be ruled," who has the queen's favor and knows it, is widely popular, and leads an army, is very "dangerous . . . to any monarch living." Bacon was warning Essex to be careful, for much as she loved him, Elizabeth could not help but see him as a threat. What was to prevent him from using his loyal soldiers against her? In turn, why shouldn't she strike against him first? At a moment, Essex might be the natural monarch to rule in the queen's declining years, or her most obvious enemy, or the key rival her heir had to either win over or defeat.

Ralegh's position was quite different. Elizabeth was his sole supporter, so he kept his focus on battling for her favor while ignoring the changes that loomed just ahead. Even when he joined the jockeying for power, it was to bring down Essex, not to ensure his own place with the next monarch.

Only one man ever learned to play well this multilayered game of treachery. This short, thin man was too frail and hunchbacked ever to fight. Sir Robert Cecil was the second son of Lord Burghley, Elizabeth's best counselor. His older brother was an extravagant wastrel. As Burghley grew old—yet another indication of changing times—he devoted a good part of his wisdom to ensuring Robert's place in the court. "I advise thee not to affect nor neglect popularity too much," he warned his son. "Seek not to be E[ssex] and shun to be R[alegh]."

Cecil was cold, calculating, and smart. Though he could never be a handsome courtier, he had just the right qualities to become an important

Robert Cecil, who outplotted Ralegh and Essex.
(COURTESY THE NATIONAL PORTRAIT GALLERY, LONDON)

adviser. While Ralegh and Essex battled each other for gold, glory, and the queen's smile, Cecil secretly plotted how to play one against the other until he alone survived.

In 1597 Essex led yet another fleet in an attempt to destroy the warships in Spain's harbors. After that they were to sail on to the Azores to capture Spanish treasure ships returning from America. His plan was to cut off the Spaniards' "golden Indian streams, whereby we shall cut his life veins and let out the vital spirits of his estate." This goal is exactly the same as what Ralegh had hoped to achieve by winning over the native Americans and capturing El Dorado: Stop the flow of New World gold and you kill the Spanish threat. Essex even hoped to land a force and capture some key Spanish cities.

The attack, led by Essex, Ralegh, and Lord Thomas Howard, failed dismally. The single success of the entire mission was vintage Ralegh, which just showed how much the rules had changed. Each captain was assigned one of islands of the Azores to attack. Ralegh was to take Fayal, but only in concert with Essex. Ralegh reached his destination on schedule and waited for Essex to arrive. His men could see the people onshore scurrying into the hills, carrying their valuables with them. For three days Ralegh held his crew back, scanning the horizon for Essex's ships.

Finally Ralegh and his cousin Sir Arthur Gorges landed and made one of their insanely brave assaults. They each wore brightly colored scarves so that the Spanish could easily see them, and they crawled directly into range of the defenders' musket fire. Both men insisted on their peacock displays, since it would be shameful "to honor the Spanish marksmen by removing their colors."

Ralegh's reckless courage won the island. But when Essex finally arrived, he threatened to courtmartial him for defying the orders and going in without him. Though he was persuaded not to hold the trial, Essex got his revenge in another way. In his report to Elizabeth he neglected to mention Ralegh's success at all. The kind of mad confidence that had once made Ralegh's reputation in Ireland was now just one more cause of friction with a powerful and deadly rival.

A disunited command trying to function in an atmosphere of poisonous competition could not make wise decisions. The English continually squabbled. They traded rumors—mainly false—about the location and aims of the Spanish gold fleet and warships, and chased after stray ships in hope of making up for past failures with new conquests. Ralegh was one of the leaders who advised against waiting for the Spanish treasure fleet, which the English wound up missing by just three hours.

While this painful comedy of errors was taking place, the Spanish were executing their own well-thought-out plan. On October 9, 1597, the dispirited English gave up on finding a vulnerable fleet and began to sail home. That very day 136 Spanish ships carrying 8,600 battle-hardened soldiers, and aided by 20 specially built landing craft, set off to attack a wholly undefended England. It would have been impossible for the splintered, tired English fleet to catch up to this fresh and well-provisioned enemy. Instead, the Spanish could have picked off the ships one by one as they tried to return to port. By October 12 the Spanish were close enough to the Lizard to map out their final assault. But that night a gale scattered the ships, and the weather grew worse day after day. Facing a foe no sailor could defeat, the Spanish gave up and turned back for home. England was safe, no thanks to any of its vain war leaders.

Essex limped back to England on October 28 and, when he heard about the armada that had just left, rushed out to capture any lingering Spanish. He swore he would get them, even if he "had to eat ropes' ends and drink nothing but rainwater." Fine words, but useless. His grand campaign had been worse than a failure, for it had opened the door to a devastating Spanish invasion. After this debacle the whole idea of attacking Spain, or stealing its American gold, lost favor.

Essex was not a man to be defeated by defeat. He just found one more arena in which to wipe away past failings with new glory. In 1599 he sailed off to Ireland to humble Catholic rebels. This was his last chance to show what a dynamic soldier could do. The Irish were too good at guerrilla warfare to engage the English directly and instead wore away at Essex's slow and ineffectual army. Once again the proud lord was disgraced. "I care not what happens to myself," he wrote in despair.

To safeguard his men, Essex made a truce with the Irish rebels that he had no power to sign. But was this really a necessary compromise? Or was Essex making secret deals in order to mount his own rebellion? No one was sure. Frantic to justify himself, he rushed back to England against Elizabeth's explicit orders, marched straight to London, and burst into her private chamber. He was "so full of dirt and mire that his very face was full of it." The startled queen, her uncombed hair wild about her, was shocked. This was such a violation of all rules that she at first did not know if he had staged a revolt and captured her castle.

What really happened in this dramatic moment? Did a lover barge into his sweetheart's bedroom, mad to prove himself? Was Essex so sure of his place as Elizabeth's love that he knew she would rather have him invade her privacy then stay at odds? Was this last bold assault—after Cádiz, and the Azores, and Ireland—the way a passionate, headstrong man showed his devotion? Or was something darker at work here? Was all the language of love a cover for a power grab by a popular general who never really accepted that England should be ruled by an aging woman rather than a dynamic man? Rumor had it that, even as he courted the queen, he called her "cankered, and her mind as crooked as her carcase."

Essex was humiliated and vulnerable, which made him all the more dangerous. He would finally have to choose: Was he the queen's suitor or her enemy? As the damaged lord flailed between reconciliation and rebellion, everyone around him plotted furiously to turn Essex's struggles to their own advantage.

Ralegh, for one, wrote to Cecil hinting that it would be a good idea for Essex to be eliminated. Quite the cold-blooded plotter, he even mapped out two alternative futures. In one Essex's legal execution would guarantee that Cecil's son could be protected against a blood feud with Essex's clan. On the other hand, if Essex stayed alive, he would destroy Cecil's entire family; "he will be able to break the branches, and pull up the [family] tree, root and all. . . . Lose not your advantage," Ralegh urged.

Essex was equally aware of the need to find his own advantage. His best chance was to negotiate an alliance with James VI, which would allow him to take on Elizabeth with his own royal backing. The sly Scottish king was interested. In their negotiations Essex made clear to the king who his enemies were in England. Chief among them were Cecil and Ralegh. While Ralegh was betraying Essex to Cecil, Essex was betraying both of them to James. Cecil was the smartest of all. In order to keep his standing with the queen, he sided with Ralegh against Essex. But there were more acts to follow, and he saw clearly what the plot would be.

Criticized and stripped of his offices by the royal council, Essex was temporarily banned from London. He was too proud and powerful a man to accept that. All could see that he was gathering disaffected people around him. On February 6, 1601, Essex and his men commissioned Shakespeare's company to perform *Richard II,* a play about deposing a bad king. The meaning of the play was obvious, even to Elizabeth. She herself had said, "I am Richard." Then Elizabeth's favorite, the great handsome soldier, turned traitor. James chose to stand back, and the bungled effort at a coup quickly failed. Under Ralegh's guidance Essex was captured, arrested for treason, tried, and killed. With him died the age of Elizabeth's court of love.

While the death of Essex would seem to be a great moment for Ralegh, it was actually a multipart disaster. Much as the two men had been rivals, they had both been favorites in an era when a queen's love could offer almost limitless wealth and power. That time was now over, and the clearest victim of the change was Ralegh, who had been continually present in all the stages of his rival's destruction. Essex had been a charismatic leader, a beloved hero. When he was executed, many felt that Ralegh, a sneaky, unpleasant favorite, had used his vile cunning to bring down a far better man. One anti-Ralegh ballad went:

> *Essex for vengeance cries*
> *His blood upon thee lies,*
> *Mounting above the skies,*
> *Damnable fiend of hell,*
> *Mischievous Matchivel!*

Ralegh was Machiavellian, but not quite enough.

As soon as Essex died, Cecil realized that he must win the favor of

James, who was the future. The best way to do that was to turn on Ralegh.

When James sent an emissary to sound out the queen's old courtier, Ralegh refused even to meet with him, feeling that this would be an offense to Elizabeth. All-trusting, Ralegh told Cecil about the overture, and Cecil urged him not to respond, nor to tell the queen. Even as he cautioned Ralegh to stay away from James, Cecil was poisoning the king's ears, warning him not to trust anything Ralegh said, whether good or bad.

Cecil used Henry Howard as his intermediary to carry messages to James. Lord Howard detested Ralegh and took every opportunity to tell the king how dangerous he was. Ralegh, he sputtered, "in pride exceedeth all men alive"; he stood "above the greatest Lucifer that hath lived in our age." Between Cecil's careful calumnies and Howard's biblical rage, the king was coming to see Ralegh as an enemy who must be eliminated.

Ralegh's only new ally in this period was Lord Cobham, a wealthy noble and engaging personality who was also a particularly weak man. Choosing a fading queen over a coming king and trusting a shallow friend instead of paying close attention to a brilliant conspirator were exceptionally bad judgments. Perhaps Ralegh really did so love the queen that he could not stand to look past her death, for even in her final days there was much to love in Elizabeth. On November 30, 1601, she gave a speech to the House of Commons that was both politically brilliant and emotionally powerful: "I do assure you there is no prince that loves his subjects better. . . . And though God hath raised me high, yet this I count the glory of my crown, that I have reigned with your loves." Her very last line was her most powerful: "Though you have had, and may have, many mightier and wiser princes sitting in this seat, yet you never had, nor shall you have any that will love you better."

Elizabeth was treating all her subjects as her courtiers, her favorites, her lovers. There was something extraordinarily humble and powerful about this. Elizabeth, the queen maiden, had forgone marriage for this special bond with her people. How could anyone in England respond but with similar devotion? Immediately, Parliament granted her a record-breaking subsidy. In the long view of history and legend she defined how any queen should rule—with and for the love of her people.

In November 1602, almost a year after her great speech, Elizabeth celebrated the forty-fourth anniversary of her accession to the throne. And she was healthy even in the early days of 1603. But by March she grew ever more melancholy and weak. In her last royal act she named James as her successor, and on March 24 she died.

Chapter 14

THE PLAY OF TREASON

Some trials are much more than tests of guilt or innocence, for in the judgment of one person's fate they dramatize the choices and challenges every human being faces. The judgment of Socrates is the most famous of these, but the trial of Sir Walter Ralegh for treason is not far behind. It was a drama on the scale of a Shakespearean tragedy. In that spirit, let us consider this chapter a treatment, a summary, for an imaginary play.

PROLOGUE: THE ROYAL HUNT

When his queen died, Ralegh finally realized what a dangerous position he was in. He rushed to meet James as the new king traveled from Edinburgh to London. According to legend, James was ready. "On my soul," he punned,

"I have heard rawly of thee." The courtier without his queen and the king on his way to claim the throne could not have been a worse match. Ralegh had used devotion to Elizabeth, courage in battle, hatred of the Spanish, and dark good looks to build a career at court. He loved tobacco and helped to popularize it. James, the son of a queen Elizabeth had ordered killed, was potbellied, scholarly, friendly to the Spanish, and suspicious. He hated tobacco and soon wrote a paper on its dangers. Each was exactly what the other was not.

James quickly showed his displeasure. He treated Ralegh as a disgraced soldier to be stripped of his rank and privileges. First the king took back Ralegh's lucrative monopolies; then he reclaimed Durham House. Without wealth or standing, what was Sir Walter, and how far would he fall? All his enemies and detractors were eager to find out.

In mid-July Ralegh was invited to Windsor Castle to join in a royal hunt. Was this a reassurance? Did it show he still mattered enough to take part in the king's games? No, for in this round of blood sport Ralegh was the real quarry.

At the castle there was no sign of danger, which was itself a sign. To capture an alert and fierce foe, you first lull him into dropping his guard. Then you use someone he trusts to lure him into your trap. One day Ralegh's false friend Cecil found him alone. He said casually enough that the king wanted him to stay and answer some questions from the royal council. That was Ralegh's last taste of true freedom. By July 20 he was in the Tower of London, held to face charges of high treason.

■ ■ ■

Ralegh in 1602, with his son Wat. (Courtesy The National Portrait Gallery, London)

ACT I: JAMES'S DOUBLE GAME

Plots, plots, and plots within plots; real treasons and imaginary ones; single, double, and triple crosses—this was the mood of London at the arrival of the new king. In this honeycomb of deceit one name came up again and again: Lord Cobham.

There was at least one real plot. Cobham's brother was entangled in a conspiracy to kidnap James and force him to shift to a more pro-Catholic policy. This was discovered before it could do much more than expose the plotters. Cobham himself was involved in another more fuzzy scheme. He didn't like James or Cecil, didn't care who knew it, and met from time to time with the ambassador from the Spanish-controlled Netherlands. Apparently they were scheming to put James's cousin Arabella Stuart on the throne in his place.

Cobham was headstrong and foolish enough not only to stumble into such conspiracies but to be obvious about it. Cobham's fumbling soon landed him in custody. But even a fool like Cobham guided by a wise old fox like Ralegh could be a threat to a king sitting on an unsteady throne. Ralegh was Cobham's close friend, and this alliance grew stronger just when the plots heated up. Ralegh had every reason to dislike James, and he had the brains to make good use of Cobham's wealth—that is, if he really was counting on such a weak and foolish man.

The punishment for treason was more than a horrible death; it also meant that the convict's family could no longer inherit his land. Instead, all his wealth reverted to the crown. There is one hint that Ralegh really was up to something. In the last months of Elizabeth's life he gave his elder son title to his estate. This was the kind of thing a careful plotter did to ensure that the land would stay in the family even if he failed. Still, the transfer was totally legal and it proved nothing.

The king had enough evidence to imprison Cobham. Now the real game started. James needed the lord to implicate Ralegh. By detaining Ralegh he had both men in his control, and he could try to scare or manipulate them until one cracked and both were sent to their doom. The king's men could interrogate each separately, control the flow of information between them, and use what they said in private, or lies about what they could have said, to get confessions. After that, the trials would be easy.

Ralegh's first responses to James's trap were similar to the double-dealing calculations he had tried with Essex and Cecil. He wrote to Cobham, and the prosecutor later claimed that this letter was designed to shut him up. Apparently it reassured the skittish lord that Ralegh had not said anything when questioned. The man who delivered it, Ralegh's lifetime friend Lawrence Keymis, may also have assured Cobham that according to law, treason needed two witnesses.

The letter has not survived, so we cannot know what Ralegh said. If the prosecutor was right, this suggests that Cobham and Ralegh did engage in some kind of treasonous talk. Years later Ralegh's son Carew claimed that his father deliberately dropped hints of disloyalty in order to smoke out real treason. Once he could identify the conspirators, he planned to turn them in. Uncovering traitors was one way to prove his loyalty, and his value, to a king inclined to suspect him. This kind of double-agent trap was used all the time by Elizabethan spies and counterspies. In *Hamlet* Shakespeare calls it the "bait of falsehood" that catches the "carp of truth." Unfortunately, Cobham was caught before Ralegh could get credit for snaring him.

Whether or not he had been toying with Cobham all along, Ralegh immediately wrote a letter to Cecil that was full of suspicion of the lord. This backfired, for Cecil, who was once again a step ahead of Ralegh, showed it to Cobham. Furious, Cobham denounced Ralegh as a traitor, only to take it back before his examiners had even gotten out of earshot.

James's game was working perfectly. Within a day Ralegh, caught in his own calculations, had provoked Cobham into making just the accusation the king needed. But Ralegh was a master of games, and his performance had just begun.

On July 21 his jailer reported Ralegh had a "mind the most dejected that ever I saw." Day after day this despairing state seemed to worsen. On July 27, just as Cecil and others came to the Tower to question prisoners, Ralegh slashed himself in the chest with a table knife. As the visitors rushed in, he burst out with a protest of his innocence.

Ralegh still thought of Cecil as his ally. He had managed to make a most dramatic case directly to the friend he hoped could help him. Cecil, though, was unconvinced. He wrote to an English ambassador, "Sir W. Ralegh attempted to have murdered himself. . . . We came to him, and found him in some agony, seeming to be unable to endure his misfortunes, and protesting innocency, with carelessness of life. In that humor he had wounded himself . . . but no way mortally, being in truth rather a cut than a stab. . . . He is very well cured, both in body and mind."

Ralegh's act should sound familiar; it was very much like what he did when he was imprisoned in Durham House and saw Elizabeth's barge pass by. Once again he made a dramatic, physical demonstration of his pain, in a way that others were sure to learn about. Yet this was more than just theatrics, for there were strong feelings behind his act. He wrote a suicide note:

All my good turns forgotten, all my errors, revived. . . . All my services, hazards, and expenses, for my Country; plantings, discoveries, fights, counsels . . . malice hath now covered over. . . . Oh intolerable infamy. Oh god I cannot resist these thoughts, I cannot live to think how I am derided, to think of the expectation of my enemies. . . . Oh death destroy my memory which is my tormentor; my thoughts and my life cannot dwell in one body.

Ralegh was being driven to the brink of suicide by the contrast between the man he tried to be and believed himself to be, and the derision, the scorn, the "expectation" of his enemies. This is an expression of anger, of injustice, of pride, not of despair. Attempting, or half attempting, suicide freed something in Ralegh. From that moment on he began to act. No longer despondent, he set himself against the power of the state.

ACT II: RALEGH TAKES CENTER STAGE

James's reasons for trying Ralegh were not limited to eliminating a potentially dangerous enemy. It did not even matter to him whether or not Ralegh was actually guilty of any treason. Publicly exposing and destroying the old courtier would confirm that the new king was in control. It would show the nation James's power, and it would warn off any any lesser men with treasonous ideas. Best of all, it would be very popular. There was a kind of symmetry. Ralegh had conspired against Essex, who was executed for treason. Now it was his turn to meet the same harsh fate.

Our legal system is based on English common law, and it is designed to prevent abuses like this, where the verdict has almost nothing to do with the actions of the accused. But English treason law in Ralegh's day was similar to that of a modern dictatorship. It served the state, not the individual. As one legal historian has put it, at that time a judge's real charge to the jury should have been, "If you acquit the prisoner, I shall be dismissed and you will go to prison. Consider your verdict."

Under the treason law of the time, the defendant was presumed guilty, not innocent. The fact that he was on trial strongly suggested that he should be. He had no right to a lawyer, nor even to know the charges against him. Only after the prosecution had made its entire case could he begin to respond to these previously unknown accusations.

Throughout the trial Ralegh protested that he should have the right to face his accuser and that no man could be convicted on just one other person's testimony. That is, he shouldn't have to face secret accusations from a single individual, who could be biased against him or in league with his enemies. He wanted to be sure that anything said against him would have to be confirmed, so that rumor or hearsay alone could not condemn him. Today Ralegh would be right on both points. But those protections are precisely what we have gained from trials like Ralegh's. His eloquence changed the rules.

In James's time there were conflicting views on how many witnesses were needed in a treason trial. But even if Ralegh had been right, the tangled law would not have done him any good. His prosecutor, Sir Edward Coke, understood that the case would hinge on exactly these rulings, and it is probable that he went over them with the judges before the trial. Coke was the greatest lawyer in England. The judges included Cecil and Henry Howard, Ralegh's secret enemies. Protest as he would, Ralegh was sure to lose. Ralegh's genius was to make the very law that doomed him the issue in the trial.

With no chance to win on the law, or to convince the jury of his inno-cence, Ralegh was trapped. Just as in Ireland when he had faced down his enemies, in the Tower when Elizabeth had imprisoned him, at Cádiz when he had challenged Essex and Admiral Charles Howard, Ralegh was at his most clear, calm, and brave when facing total defeat.

On November 17 the crowd got their revenge on the man they hated. As Ralegh was taken on the five-day trip from the Tower to Winchester for his trial, he was mobbed. People yelled at him, screamed their anger, and pelted him with stones, mud, even tobacco pipes. His jailer wasn't sure they could make it to the court. "It was hab or nab whether Sir Walter Ralegh should have been brought alive through such multitudes of unruly people as did exclaim against him." Sir Walter ignored the tumult and smoked his pipe.

It was that same cool clarity that won the day. Though Coke had every-thing going for him, he still seemed to fear Ralegh. He kept overstating Ralegh's crimes, accusing him of anything and everything, making him out to be "a spider of hell," the worst monster in England. Faced with such curses, Ralegh demonstrated to the court and to posterity the fate of an innocent man fighting the monster of the state.

> COKE: I will then come close to you. I will prove you to be the most notori-ous traitor that ever came to the bar. . . .
>
> RALEGH: Your words cannot condemn me. My innocency is my defense. Prove against me any one thing of the many that you have broken, and I will confess all the indictment, and that I am the most horrible traitor that ever lived, and worthy to be crucified with a thousand torments.
>
> COKE: Nay, I will prove all. Thou art a monster. Thou has an English face, but a Spanish heart.

The cornerstone of the king's case was that Ralegh was in league with the hated Spanish. But Coke's effort to keep reinforcing that connection gave Ralegh a chance to remind everyone of his brave efforts against the same enemy. Reviewing his many battles against Spain on land and sea, in Ireland, at Cádiz, Ralegh took his listeners back to his part in the glorious reign of Elizabeth, "a Lady whom time had surprised."

Ralegh's gracious bow to the queen's memory must have moved the crowd. And he had a much more subtle way to use popular hatred of Spain: "If you proceed to condemn me by bare inferences, without an oath . . . without witness, upon paper accusations, you try me by the Spanish inquisition."

How brilliant, for instead of being tainted by association with the enemy, Ralegh made everyone in court see that the English government was acting like the worst of the Spanish. Now he was the victim, not the villain, and everyone could identify with him. He made sure everyone would:

> I will . . . expect nothing of you but what reason, religion, and conscience ask for every man: only this let me say to every one of you in particular;—remember what St. Augustine saith, "So judge as if you were about to be judged yourself, for in the end there is but one Judge and one Tribunal for all men." Before that Tribunal both you and I must stand. Now if you yourselves would like to be hazarded in your lives . . . your lands, goods, and all you have confiscated, your wives, children and servants left crying to the world . . . without the open testimony of a single witness, then so judge me as you would yourselves be judged!

After Ralegh's stirring speech, Coke grew ever more frantic and cruel, while the supposed traitor came across as ever more sincere and human:

RALEGH: Mr. Attorney, have you done?

COKE: Yes, if you have no more to say.

RALEGH: If you have done, then I have somewhat more to say.

COKE: Nay, I will have the last word for the King.

RALEGH: Nay, I will have the last word for my life.

Any listener could identify with Ralegh speaking to defend his life and could not miss Coke's sputtering, bullying tone. The very inequality of the trial now stood in Ralegh's favor. Exposed, alone, threatened, he stood for everyone in England. If James's henchmen could destroy him, who was next?

Despite all his eloquence, Ralegh lost. He lost on the law. He lost on the poker play of Cobham's written statements—Ralegh's surprise revelation was that he had managed to sneak out a retraction from his former friend. The prosecution's better surprise was that it possessed a later retraction of the retraction. He lost in court when the handpicked judges and the cowed jury did finally convict him.

Worst of all, he lost everything in Chief Justice Popham's sentence:

> Sir Walter Ralegh, since you have been found guilty of these horrible treasons, the judgment of the court is, that you shall be . . . drawn upon a hurdle through the open streets to the place of execution, there to be hanged and cut down alive, and your body shall be opened, your heart and bowels plucked out, and your privy members cut off and thrown in the fire before your eyes. Then your head to be stricken from your body, and your body shall be divided into four quarters, to be disposed of at the king's pleasure.

And yet Ralegh actually won. His eloquence in defense of the individual against the state was so magnificent that it won the crowd and even the court. One observer wrote:

Sir Walter Ralegh served for a whole act, and played all the parts himself. . . . He answered with that temper, wit, learning, courage, and judgment, that, save it went with the hazard of his life, it was the happiest day that ever he spent. And so well he shifted all advantages that were taken against him, that . . . in the opinion of all men, he had been acquitted.

"Never," another courtier concluded, "was a man so hated and so popular, in so short a time."

James was like a spider. He liked to keep out of sight, but he remained in touch, tied to everything that was going on through spies and messengers. One spy at the trial told him that "whereas when he saw [Ralegh] first he was so led with the common hatred, that he would have gone a hundred miles to have seen him hanged, he would, ere he parted, have gone a thousand to have saved his life." Even the king now knew that the trial had turned Ralegh from the people's enemy into a popular hero.

Coke, Cecil, and Howard, all acting for James's sake, had held a show trial to demonstrate the king's power. Ralegh stole the show. For the first time all England saw the courtier Elizabeth had admired. This was a uniquely bold, brilliant, and decisive person. At his best he was the voice of all men.

Sir Walter was a convicted traitor, yet this was not the end of the play. There was still one more act to come.

Act III: Plays Within Plays

There were many kinds of theater in Ralegh's life: royal pageants and court chivalry; plots and schemes and double crosses; great speeches by Elizabeth to her people; spectacular battles that played like epic entertainments. And, of course, there were the plays of Shakespeare and his contemporaries, which transformed all this into enduring drama. Ralegh's trial was no exception.

Most of the men convicted in Cobham's various plots were to be executed on December 10, 1603. Though Ralegh's date was not yet set, he could see the scaffold from his cell. The king planned the execution as a play, for he had secretly pardoned the men. But his messenger was instructed not to announce this until the very last moment. They were to believe they would die, and then they would be saved. On the day of the event the king's man arrived late and had to rush through the crowd. He barely made it in time to tell each man that he had been spared, temporarily.

According to an observer, standing together on the scaffold the prisoners "looked strange one upon the other, like men beheaded and met again in the other world. Now all the actors being together on the stage (as use is at the end of a play)." Ralegh had been both audience and participant in this drama of death delayed. In time his pardon followed.

Ralegh had played to the crowd and won their praise. James used his turn at stage-managing to play a sadistic game with the convicts. He may have scared them into obedience, but people now associated him with cruel scheming.

That Christmas the king held his first holiday revels. On December 26, 1603, the king's players put on the very first royal performance of Shakespeare's *Hamlet*. The play is about many things, including what it means to act and to play a part. Hamlet is a prince whose father was killed by the very man who now sits on the throne, his uncle Claudius. In the second act Hamlet plots to put on a play that will remind Claudius of his crime, so that he will give away his guilt. Hamlet says, "The play's the thing/Wherein I'll catch the conscience of the king."

In the second scene of the third act Hamlet stages his show, "The Murder of Gonzago." Think of the scene that night at the Great Hall of the royal residence, Hampton Court. At the rear of the stage actors playing the evil king and weak queen of Denmark faced out to the audience. In front of them was the play within the play, all about a second set of guilty kings and queens. Facing the actors directly, in an exact mirror of the arrangement onstage, sat James and his wife, Queen Anne of Denmark. Who could avoid noticing the parallel?

Exactly one year later Shakespeare's men performed their new play, *Measure for Measure*, for the king. In it the playwright criticized a cruel state in which even understandable offenses were punishable by death. Like James, Duke Vincentio of Vienna in the play disliked crowds. In turn, the common people yearned for the leniency of an earlier day. Shakespeare's play commented on the show trial and mock execution James had staged and Ralegh had stolen.

Measure for Measure caught a mood of dislike for the king's harsh rule. For years after there were rumors that the judges and jurors in the Ralegh trial had made deathbed confessions, regretting their actions. Even if these were more legend than fact, they matched the popular feeling. James's wife and his older son, ten-year-old Henry, responded more directly to Ralegh's brilliant performance. They turned to him for advice. The imprisoned man, who was supposed to be killed in the most cruel and public manner possible as an example of the new king's power, soon became the beloved tutor of the prince of the realm.

Through his words and his courage, Sir Walter Ralegh had saved his own life and given himself hope for the future. Coke later had his own falling-out with James and, in his highly influential law books, defended the very rights Ralegh had spoken for in court. It is not far-fetched to say that Ralegh so challenged the treason laws of his time that our rights are protected to this day.

Chapter 15

THE STORY OF OUR DAYS

The greatest accomplishment of the Elizabethans may have been the way they turned their adventurous and theatrical lives into words. For thirteen years after his conviction Ralegh was a prisoner in the Tower of London. There he led a full life, seeing his wife and family, conducting chemical experiments, giving advice to friends and members of the court. Most importantly, he wrote.

There was a repeated pattern in Ralegh's life. He would try some bold action, such as spreading his cape before the queen or sending a colony to North America or sailing in search of El Dorado. Though always full of promise, the effort would not quite work out as he hoped. Then he, or a close friend, would write about it. Each time, a bold act became eloquent prose. On paper, after the fact, he transformed passion, hope, even despair, into enduring literature.

For five years, from 1609 to 1614, Ralegh worked on a huge book, his *History of the World*. He had become Henry's tutor a year or two before he began it, and he wrote it "for the service of that inestimable prince." It does not resemble anything we would call world history today. In six volumes he covered only from biblical creation to Rome's wars with Carthage. And his opinions are nothing like the balanced judgments we expect in history texts. He was giving examples from the long history of mankind to instruct a prince in how to act. That was what made it so popular. The history went through ten editions in the seventeenth century, and remained in print through almost all of the twentieth. Ralegh gave history a pattern; he

The title page and an image of the author from Ralegh's History of the World. While the map of the world is still centered on the Holy Land, the continents have been filled in, and every place is important. (COURTESY IAN MAXTED)

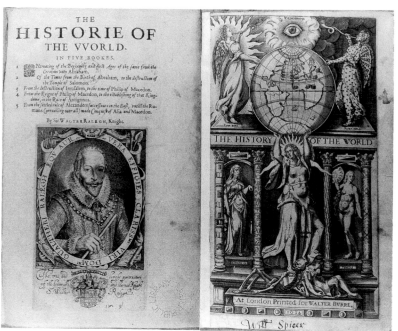

Ralegh as an older man. A map of Cádiz, scene of one of his greatest triumphs, hangs behind him. His injury in that battle forced him to use a cane. The sash on his left arm shows his importance, perhaps for his past triumphs or because he is about to set off, again, for El Dorado.

showed how it made sense. For a religious people who were nonetheless experiencing great change, this was very appealing.

Starting with the Bible, Ralegh explained the past in two different ways. On the one hand, he traced out the causes and effects of individual actions. Just as in his poem "The Lie," he had a sharp and cynical eye on how every person scrambles after his own advantage. On the other hand, he demonstrated over and over again how everything was the will of God, which should encourage faith and humility.

Discussing the origin of government, for example, Ralegh explained that "though (speaking humanely) the beginning of Empire may be ascribed to reason and necessity; yet it was God himself that first kindled this light in the minds of men." This is just the balance of human and divine causation Shakespeare put in *Hamlet:* "There's a divinity that shapes our ends,/ Rough-hew them how we will."

By stressing divine judgment as well as human will, Ralegh also got across a more subtle and dangerous message. He showed in the safe examples of biblical stories and long-dead rulers the fate of bad kings. Written to instruct the heir to England's throne, Ralegh's history was one long indictment of King James.

A thinly disguised challenge to an unpopular king was a limited risk because Ralegh knew he had powerful allies, including the best of all, Henry. The prince complained that "no king but my father would keep such a bird in a cage." Once he came to power, Henry planned to first free, then reward the man whom he had come to trust and admire. James disliked and eventually banned Ralegh's history. But for the royal heir it was just the written form of his favorite lessons. Like almost all of Ralegh's plots, however, this one, too, nearly succeeded and then utterly failed. For in 1612

Prince Henry died, and with him died Ralegh's path to regaining all he had lost.

ENDGAME

Ralegh and James were by now cunning, tired old enemies playing out the end of a long, unpleasant game. Like chess masters down to their final pieces, they could neither escape nor defeat each other. Ralegh was too popular for the king to kill. But the king was the king, and unless something radically changed, Sir Walter would end his days trapped in the Tower of London. Each watched the other, waiting for the enemy to weaken.

From 1614 on, James got into ever deeper financial trouble. The Crown owed a great deal of money. The normal and legal way for a king to get new funds was to request them from Parliament. This is what Elizabeth managed to do so well in her Golden Speech. Then, by stressing her love for her people, she persuaded their representatives to raise even more money than she had requested. It was exactly this link between ruler and subject that Ralegh praised in his history, and it was precisely this kind of rule that James could not stand. He hated the idea of humbling himself to Parliament and tried to govern without it. But if he was not going to get money from his subjects, he would have to find it another way. This gave Ralegh one last opening, a final chance to get out of check, and perhaps deliver his own mating blow.

Year after year Ralegh kept track of what was going on in the Americas. Though his patent had lapsed and he had taken no part in establishing the Jamestown colony, it was the clear successor to his previous ventures. The settlement was in the very Chesapeake site he favored, and the plan for the colony was based on what people had learned from his mistakes.

North America was in new hands, so he paid special attention to ships that returned to places where he had gone in search for gold. A series of expeditions inspired by his own report had revisited the Orinoco. The most important trip came in 1610–11, when Sir Thomas Roe reached deep enough into the continent to establish once and for all that there was no Manoa. But he also reported Spanish activity at the junction of the Orinoco and the Caroni rivers, just where Ralegh thought there must be a gold mine.

A desperate king could not afford to dismiss any rumor, and a desperate prisoner could not pass up any chance for freedom. Ralegh sent word of the Spanish gold waiting to be claimed for England. If he could just be freed to find the mine he believed was there, James would be a wealthy king.

James's pride and the poverty it produced gave Ralegh his release. The king agreed to let him gather ships and men and sail back to Guiana. Score one for Ralegh, who stood to find a fortune, or escape to friendly parts of Holland or France if he did not. Still, James was not yet ready to accept defeat. Ralegh was released with two very strict conditions. He was to return with gold. But, on pain of death, he was not to harm the Spanish in any way. James then told the powerful Spanish ambassador exactly where Ralegh planned to go.

The Spanish had had arms and fortifications on the Orinoco even when Ralegh made his first trip up the river. Over the next two decades they had strengthened their position. Ralegh's charge was to steal in past them and bring back gold that they somehow had neglected to find. That would have been hard under any conditions. James did his best to make it very nearly impossible.

As with Cecil, Ralegh calculated and schemed to outthink his enemies, only to be totally outthought by them. His very play for final freedom sent him directly into a final trap.

Proving a Myth

There was something appropriate even about this last blind alley, for it permitted Ralegh to be the one to complete the quest for El Dorado. To prove can mean to test. "The exception proves the rule" really means that a rule that does not explain the exception has been proved false. Read this way, as Ralegh often used it, to prove means to challenge, to "put the lie," and thus to discover the truth.

Ralegh's last voyage proved the myth of El Dorado, and exposed it for what it was: a European dream that had become a nightmare, a madness, a questing after phantoms that only grew ever more destructive the more hopeless it became. There were no golden kingdoms left in the continent of South America; there were only tangles of legends and lies in the minds of would-be conquerors. Ralegh gave more than his life to make this final proof, which is why he is a true tragic hero.

The trip was a wrong turn into hell. Leading a fleet of some twenty boats was a ship with the apt name of the *Destiny*. On it were Ralegh, his son Walter (called Wat), and his loyal friend Keymis. While crossing the ocean Ralegh contracted a violent fever, and he was too weak to go on the actual expedition in search of the mine. That left it to Wat and Keymis to lead the men upriver. Taking after his father, Wat was bold to the point of being reckless. Told not to engage with the Spanish, he attacked a Spanish fort and was killed instantly. Some Spaniards also fell, which only made it worse. Not only was Ralegh's older son dead, but by fighting and killing the Spanish he had violated the terms of his father's release. Now there was no hope at all.

When Keymis returned to tell his tale, Ralegh could not stand to hear it. There was no mine and no gold; his son was dead; he faced certain death back home. Ralegh raged at the man who had been his most devoted ally. Keymis went to his room and killed himself. Rather than bringing freedom or fortune, the search for the golden kingdom had destroyed the deepest bonds and fondest hopes. When Ralegh wrote to tell his wife about the disaster, he could barely find words: "My brains are broken, and so it is a torment for me to write." His sole counsel was to "obey the will and providence of God," and his only comfort was that he expected his own death to come soon.

This was the sure and final proof that there was no El Dorado. There was absolutely nothing to be found along the black rivers but the delusions Europeans had brought with them.

Sharp Medicine

Ralegh could have fled. He had offers of safety from the French. But he rejected them and headed back to meet his fate. When he reached London, though, he seemed to have second thoughts. Assisted by his jailer, Sir Lewis Stuckley, he donned a false beard and boarded a small boat that could take him to France. This last hope was really a final betrayal, for the boat was being shadowed by a larger craft carrying the king's men. Stuckley had set up the whole plan in order to catch Ralegh in one last crime, the effort to flee.

There could be no escape this time. In killing the Spaniards in America, Ralegh had violated the king's order, and he demonstrated his criminality by trying to get away from his jailer. Of course none of this made any sense. In 1603 he had been convicted for conspiring with the Spanish, then in 1618 he was condemned under that very indictment for fighting against them. He chose to return to England when he had all of the ocean before him, only to be trapped into trying to escape across the channel. Still, for new crimes or old, he was sure to be executed. One last time, when faced with death, he was grand.

On the night before his execution, Ralegh copied an old poem of his, and added two last lines as a new ending.

> *Even such is time, which takes in trust*
> *Our youth, our joys, and all we have,*
> *And pays us but with age, and dust;*
> *Who in the dark and silent grave*
> *When we have wandered all our ways*
> *Shuts up the story of our days.*
> *And from which earth and grave and dust,*
> *The Lord will raise me up I trust.*

The last performance in Sir Walter Ralegh's life of epic adventure was his death. He showed how a strong and courageous person meets his fate. Ralegh really believed everything he wrote about accepting the will of God. With his final act he made sure everybody saw that.

On Friday, October 29, 1618, he walked to the scaffold. Seeing an old man in the crowd, Ralegh asked why he was there. "Nothing but to see you, and to pray God to have mercy on your soul," he replied. Ralegh made a presentation of his hat, saying, "Thou hast more need of it now than I."

He then gave a long speech, defending himself against the most recent charges and even returning to his struggle with Essex. Though they had been rivals, he wanted to make sure no one thought he had enjoyed Essex's execution. When he was finally alone with the executioner, he gave away what he had in his pockets and asked to see the ax. Casually, theatrically, he ran his finger along the blade. "This is sharp medicine," he joked, "but it is a sure cure for all diseases." Refusing the blindfold that would have hidden the shadow of the falling ax, he lay there waiting to die. When even the executioner hesitated, Ralegh urged him on: "What dost thou fear? Strike, man, strike!"

And so he did.

It took a man of Ralegh's great spirit to seek paradise and to fail. Though his life was at times brutal, was often frustrating, and ended with tragedy, he left behind an important legacy. He was the bridge between the Old World and the New. In his words and his deeds he pointed the way to the land across the seas. If he never found his El Dorado, his writings described the force of his yearning for that conquest and the counterforce of the beauty of the new land. Perhaps it is fitting that he never succeeded in creating a settlement here, for he was poised precisely between one world and the other.

Yet in another way he had already crossed over. Ralegh's constant striving to rise in a rigid society made him a terror in Ireland and a patron in

North America. For every dark trait of his that people disliked, there was a strength to admire. It is this flawed humanity that makes him appealing. He was no saint and no devil. The massacre he led and the tolerance he supported, his calculations at court and his deep disdain for society's lies, his searching questions and profound faith—in all these contradictions he was our true ancestor, the first modern man.

"There is a spirit that is seeking through America for Raleigh;
in the earth, the air, the waters, up and down, for Raleigh, that lost man:
seer who failed, planter who never planted,
poet whose works are questioned, leader without command, favorite deposed—
but one who yet gave title for his Queen, his England,
to a coast he never saw but grazed alone with genius."
—William Carlos Williams

Endnotes and Bibliography

Searching the Internet for Sir Walter Ralegh (with and without the *i* in his last name) with any good search engine will lead to many sites. The best I've found has a long address but is worth the effort. Jim Batten has created a central Ralegh home page with links that take you to a wide variety of other places, including sites that have some of his best poems. All sites, though, should be treated as sources that need to be checked, evaluated, and compared with other sources, such as this book. Jim's site is:

www.devon-cc.gov.uk/tourism/pages/woodbury/raleigh.html.

NOTE TO READERS

John Manningham's poem/puzzle can be found in Agnes M. C. Latham, ed., *The Poems of Sir Walter Ralegh* (London: Constable, 1929), page 69. Latham's is the most complete collection of his poetry, but it uses his original spelling and can be hard to follow.

PROLOGUE:
BETWEEN PARADISE AND THE SERPENT'S MOUTH

p. 1　　Ralegh's description of his desperate condition is from his own account of his trip in search of El Dorado. I have much more to say about the trip and his account of it in chapter 11. See Walter Ralegh, *The Discoverie of the Large, Rich and Bewtiful Empyre of Guiana* (London, 1596; facsimile edition, New York: Da Capo, 1968), page 89; Columbus is quoted in a marvelous book by H. J. Mozans (pseudonym for John A. Zahm) called *Up the Orinoco and Down the Magdalena* (New York: Appleton, 1910), pages 65, 68. The author took the trip his title suggested near the turn of the century. His appreciation of the indigenous peoples and his criticism of and suspicion of old European accounts are quite modern and refreshing. The book is both easy to read and filled with fascinating details.

p. 2   For the "mighty" storm, his indecision, and his trust in God, see *Discoverie*, page 89.

p. 3   For the date when the El Dorado story was recorded, as well as more generally for this entire chapter, see John Hemming, *The Search for El Dorado* (London: Book Club Associates, 1978), page 97. Other sources mention earlier dates, but Hemming's book is the most thorough that I've seen. It is well written and filled with maps and black-and-white and color photos. The book recounts many great tales of adventure and is a treat for all readers.

p. 8   I found this extract from Donne's "Elegy" in Charles Nicholl, *The Creature in the Map: A Journey to El Dorado* (New York: Morrow, 1995), page 166. I found Nicholl very useful in researching chapter 11 and have more to say about him in the notes for those pages.

RISING

p. 11   Sir Robert Naunton's image of Ralegh as fortune's "Tennis-Ball" is from Willard Mosher Wallace, *Sir Walter Raleigh* (Princeton, New Jersey: Princeton University Press, 1959), page 5. This is a fine biography aimed at adults but accessible to young readers.

CHAPTER 1: FROM DEVON TO THE WARS

p. 13   This description of Ralegh's birthplace is based on the excellent adult biography by Robert Lacey, *Sir Walter Ralegh* (London: Weidenfeld, 1973), page 15. Additional information comes courtesy of Jim Batten, a wonderfully informed and helpful government official in Devon, at JBatten@www.devon-cc.gov.uk.

p. 14   John Aubrey was born shortly after Ralegh died, and he based his account of Ralegh on the word of people who knew him. While he isn't always trustworthy, we are sure he got the accent right. His line is quoted in A. L. Rowse, *Sir Walter Ralegh, His Family and Private Life* (New York: Harper, 1962), page 134. [Rowse wrote a number of well-researched and readable books on this period: I give full listings on first use, then use initials. This is now *SWR*.] Essex's disdainful remarks are also in Rowse, *SWR*, on page 129.

On the Tangier Islanders, see Robert McCrum, William Cran, and Robert MacNeil, *The Story of English* (New York: Viking, 1986), pages 107–8. This engaging book accompanied a TV series and is designed to interest a large audience.

p. 15   Shakespeare on order is from his *Troilus and Cressida,* Act I, Scene 3, and appears in E. M. W. Tillyard, *The Elizabethan World Picture* (New York: Vintage Books), page 9. This book assumes a base of knowledge on the part of the reader, but is both fascinating and concise. It explains the balance of old order and new disruption in Elizabeth's time very well.

Marlowe's *Tamburlaine* is quoted in John Hale, *The Civilization of Europe in the Renaissance* (New York: Simon & Schuster, 1993), page 19. Again, this is for readers who have some knowledge of the period, but it has a wealth of interesting stories and examples.

p. 16   For this history of English maps, see A. L. Rowse, *The England of Elizabeth: The Structure of Society* (London: Reprint Society, 1950) [hereafter *EE*] pages 68, 71.

Sir Thomas More is quoted in John Guy, "The Tudor Age," in Kenneth O. Morgan, ed., *The Oxford Illustrated History of Britain* (Oxford: Oxford University Press, 1981), page 242.

p. 17   On the changes in English, see *The Story of English*, page 95.

Aubrey on printing is quoted in Oliver Lawson Dick's introduction to *John Aubrey, Brief Lives* (London: Secker and Warburg, 1949), page xxxiii.

p. 20   In general for the background of Protestantism and Catholicism and Ralegh's family, see Lacey, pages 15–19.

p. 21   These dates for Ralegh's youth can be found in Wallace on page 69.

Aubrey's account of these comments on Ralegh at Oxford can be found in every standard biography. There is no way to know if Aubrey actually heard them from people who knew Ralegh, or if they remembered correctly. But they sound just about right.

p. 23   Ralegh's comments on the war, from his *History of the World*, can be found in Lacey, pages 22–23

This summary of the French wars of religion comes from J. H. M. Salmon, *Society in Crisis: France in the Sixteenth Century* (New York: St. Martin's, 1975), pages 186–87, a clear but certainly scholarly work for those who want to study the subject in detail.

pp. 24–25   Thomas Fuller's *The Worthies of England* (London: 3.G.W.L. and W.G., 1662), pages 261–62; Fuller was a preacher and supporter of royalty who lived in the first half of the seventeenth century. The book that told this story was published the year after he died, in 1662. He was related by marriage to the man who attended to Ralegh in his last hours in prison, so he could have heard the story from him. But since there is no other source, the story could also be apocryphal. Like Parson Weems's fable of young George Washington and the cherry tree, it could be an invented tale that served to illustrate the kind of man Ralegh turned out to be. Most standard biographies use Fuller's story but alter it for dramatic effect. If we follow his original edition, the cape and window were two different events.

p. 25   On the seal, see Walter Fraser Oakeshott, *The Queen and the Poet* (New York: Barnes & Noble, 1961), pages 22, 23. Oakeshott explains why the 1584 we see in the seal is actually 1585 by modern reckoning, and also weighs other possible meanings of the cloak. This is an intelligent, engaged discussion of Ralegh's poetry in the context of his life. The comments are at college level, though the poetry is easier to read than in some other books because he modernizes the spelling and adds explanatory notes.

CHAPTER 2: THE QUEEN'S PROBLEM

pp. 27–28   For a clear, though quite detailed and somewhat academic, explanation of Elizabeth and the issue of marriage, see Susan Doran, *Monarchy and Matrimony: The Courtships of Elizabeth I* (New York: Routledge, 1996). On pages 6–12 Doran describes the various theories that historians have offered on why Elizabeth did not marry. Unlike others who see psychological damage or feminist courage and calculation in Elizabeth, she argues that the queen actually wanted to marry and came close to doing so on a number of occasions. While making use of her excellent research, I have chosen to present the marriage issue as more about Elizabeth's way of ruling than the power of factions at court.

For a good book on Elizabeth aimed at younger readers, see Jane Resh Thomas, *Behind the Mask: The Life of Queen Elizabeth I* (New York: Clarion Books, 1998).

Doran mentions Henry's very early plans for Elizabeth on page 13.

Doran offers this wonderful quotation from the Spanish ambassador on page 22.

pp. 30–37 This whole section is a close paraphrase of a detailed but readable study that has a wealth of information and is worth reading for anyone interested in a progress: Zillah Dovey, *An Elizabethan Progress: The Queen's Journey into East Anglia, 1578* (Madison, New Jersey: Fairleigh Dickinson University Press, 1996). The Spanish ambassador is on page 1.

p. 32 For Leicester and the Hatton story, see J. E. Neale, *Queen Elizabeth* (New York: Harcourt, Brace, 1934), pages 211–12. Though the language of this book contains old-fashioned assumptions about men and women and concentrates very heavily on politics, it is a clear, well-written, and quite thoroughly researched biography. In addition, it is the basis for many recent books. Worth dipping into for its rich sources. For Walsingham, see Ann Somerset, *Elizabeth I* (London: Weidenfeld, 1991), page 278. This is a recent biography that relies on Neale and other sources and has a more modern tone. For Burghley, see Rowse, *EE*, page 316.

p. 32 For the start of the progress, see Dovey, pages 21–23.

pp. 32–36 For the Cambridge debate, see Dovey, page 34; Ascham is quoted in Neale, page 16. For the Norwich preparations, see Dovey, pages 63–65. For the queen's arrival, see Dovey, pages 66–68. For her entry into the city, see Dovey, page 69. This wonderful Mercury is described in Dovey, page 75. For this praise of chastity, see Dovey, page 77. On the hunt, see Somerset, page 381. For the quaking schoolmaster, see Dovey, page 79.

CHAPTER 3: PLANTATIONS

p. 38   For "scalding fire," see "A Poem Put into My Lady Laiton's Pocket by Sir W. Ralegh" in Latham, page 74.

p. 39   The patent is cited in Lacey, page 28.

An excellent summary of Gilbert's expeditions and the link to Ireland, and a short, readable, well-researched introduction to all of Ralegh's overseas efforts, is David B. Quinn, *Raleigh and the British Empire* (London: The English Universities Press, 1947; new edition, 1962), pages 28–31. [Since Quinn has written a number of excellent books on Ralegh and exploration, I will give a complete listing on first use, then refer to each by its initials. This one is now *RBE*.]

p. 40   This summary of English aims in Ireland can be found in Thomas E. Hachey, Joseph M. Hernon, Jr., and Lawrence J. McCaffrey, *The Irish Experience: A Concise History*, revised ed. (Armonk, New York: M. E. Sharp, 1996), page 16.

Bacon is quoted in A. L. Rowse, *The Expansion of Elizabethan England* (New York: Scribner, 1972), page 90 [hereafter *EofEE*].

p. 40   This extract from Spenser is quoted and interpreted as being about the Irish in Rowse, *EofEE*, page 129.

p. 41   For the Williams quote, see *Irish Experience*, page 19.

p. 41   Ralegh on fighting for homeland is cited in Lacey, page 34.

pp. 41–45   The conflicting histories of the Smerwick massacre are themselves an indication of the passions of Irish history. There are only a few primary sources: English state papers pertaining to Ireland; a letter to Elizabeth from Lord Grey; an Irish chronicle that was appended to an English compilation; Irish oral history, preserved in what is called the *History of Catholic Ireland;* letters to and from Spain about the event; papers preserved by a relative of Ralegh's, Sir George Carew. And yet accounts drawn from these limited sources vary greatly: Were there six hundred, seven hundred, eight hundred mercenaries? Were they mainly Italian ruffians or Spanish soldiers? After some left, did two hundred Irish join them? Were there women among these Irish? Pregnant women? On which day did the fort surrender? Why? Did Ralegh join in the killing or not?

Yet even if the details are blurred, the outline is clear: The Catholic forces surrendered and were killed. At the least, Ralegh sanctioned cold-blooded killing. At the most, he directed it. Eleanor Hull, *A History of Ireland and Her People* (London: Harrap, 1926–31), pages 381–83; Cyril Bentham Falls, *Elizabeth's Irish Wars* (London: Methuen, 1950), pages 142–45; Lacey tells the story but allows for the chance that Grey did not betray his promise, page 37; Wallace is less willing to consider excuses, pages 16–17; Quinn, *RBE*, pages 33–34, is not sure Ralegh participated in the killing and stresses that he was under orders. The first two mention November 9; Quinn, November 10. All agree, though, that joining in the massacre precisely fits the character of a man whose youth had been spent in horrific religious warfare.

pp. 45–46   For the gallant phase of Ralegh in Ireland, see Wallace, page 18.

CHAPTER 4: FORTUNE'S FAVOR

pp. 47–48   On the portrait, see Somerset, insert after page 372; on hands, page 64; on gems, see comments on the same painting in Stephen J. Greenblatt, *Sir Walter Ralegh: The Renaissance Man and His Roles* (New Haven: Yale University Press, 1973), page 75. Greenblatt's book had a strong influence on my thinking and even helped define what I wanted to get at in this book. He is well known in academic circles as a leading practitioner of a school of literary and cultural analysis called New Historicism. New Historicists try to find traces of larger social trends in artworks and, in reverse, seek keys to the larger society through close analysis of artists' images. That view was quite popular in the 1980s and 1990s when I was in graduate school, and English majors are sure to encounter it in college. But it has also been challenged. Charles Nicholl offers some counterviews to Greenblatt. As a historian, I have found New Historicist studies fascinating and suggestive but very hard to prove. Many also tend to associate social analysis with Marxist critique, which can be useful but also limiting.

p. 49   For the smoke bet and Elizabeth's remark, see Lacey, page 90.

For Diana, see Oakeshott, pages 148–49.

p. 50   Aubrey can be found in Lacey, page 52.

p. 51 For the figures, see Lacey, page 53. Lacey adds the two grants and arrives at earnings of just under a million, but his book was published in 1973. Allowing for inflation, Ralegh probably was a millionaire.

For "reaps," see Wallace, page 11.

Ralegh in Devon and as a tough manager follows Lacey, pages 53–54; Aubrey on Ralegh's pride is quoted in Wallace, page 25. For his defiance, see Fuller, page 262.

THE LOST COLONY

p. 53 Ralegh on new worlds is from his "The XIth and Last Book of the Ocean to Cynthia" in Oakeshott, page 179. The long title alludes to ten other "books," but scholars agree that he wrote only this one.

CHAPTER 5: NEAR TO HEAVEN BY SEA

p. 55 This picture of Durham House is a composite from what follows, and also a somewhat similar image in David Quinn, *Set Fair for Roanoke: Voyages and Colonies, 1584–1606* (Chapel Hill: University of North Carolina Press, 1985), page 149 [hereafter *SF*]. In this book, written for the four hundredth anniversary of the first colony, Quinn revisits many of his earlier studies, adding the most current thinking on each issue. It is a very good single-volume summary of what we know about the lost colony, what questions remain, and what kinds of research are likely to prove most useful.

Lacey estimates Ralegh's contribution on page 55; on Gilbert and Ralegh, Quinn, *RBE*, page 43.

p. 56 For Elizabeth on Gilbert, see Lacey, page 56.

Lacey recounts this story on page 56. He does not make clear who described the "terrible seas."

For the suggestion that Gilbert was reading More, see Samuel Eliot Morison, *The European Discovery of America* (New York: Oxford University Press, 1971–74), page 577.

The patent is cited in Lacey, page 55.

p. 57   This great extract comes to us courtesy of Lacey, page 57.

pp. 57–59   On Dee in general, see Lacey, page 50; for Dee and Gilbert, see David B. Quinn, *North America from Earliest Discovery to First Settlements: The Norse Voyages to 1612* (New York: Harper, 1977) [hereafter *NA*], page 376; on what the New World may have meant to Dee, see Nicholl, pages 306–7. In that passage Nicholl is talking about Ralegh's later explorations in Guiana, but it applies to Dee's, and perhaps Ralegh's, views of all American exploration.

p. 60   On Hariot, see also Ralph C. Staiger, *Thomas Harriot: Science Pioneer* (New York: Clarion Books, 1998).

CHAPTER 6: A LAND OF PLENTY

p. 61   On the need for a midpoint landing, see Quinn, *NA*, page 325.

p. 62   Barlowe on the land is quoted in Quinn, *RBE*, page 52.

p. 63   Barlowe on the natives is from Quinn, *SF*, page 212.

Barlowe on the corn and natives is from Quinn, *RBE*, pages 54–55.

p. 64   For the real story behind the myth of abundance, see Quinn, *RBE*, pages 56–58.

pp. 64–65   For the makeup of the second expedition, see Quinn, *RBE*, page 65; Quinn gives an alternative spelling of Ganz as Dougham Gannes in *SF*, page 92; Morison finds the *Tiger* in *Macbeth*, Act I, Scene 3, on page 627.

p. 65   For these initial misfortunes, see Quinn, *NA*, page 329.

p. 69   For White's promising and Amadas's destructive encounters, see Quinn, *RBE*, page 70.

pp. 69–70   On Lane, see Quinn, *RBE*, page 75; Quinn, *SF*, points out that White, who counted 108 total, forgot to include himself.

p. 70   Hariot is quoted in Quinn, *SF*, page 89.

pp. 70–71   For Lane's famous assessment, see Quinn, *SF*, page 147.

p. 71   Quinn discusses Lane's feelings about the natives, which included a kind of rough admiration, in *SF* on page 219.

p. 73   Quinn tells the story of the possible blacks and South Americans left behind in *SF* on page 343.

      For Hariot on Wingina, see Quinn, *SF,* page 227.

      For Hariot on ingenuity, see Quinn *SF,* page 222.

p. 75   For Hariot's amazing perception of two kinds of superstition, see *Thomas Hariot's Virginia* (March of America Facsimile Series, #15, Ann Arbor University Microfilms, 1966 facsimile of Theodore de Bry's 1590 edition), page 29.

p. 76   For "civilized," see Hariot, *Virginia,* page 25.

Chapter 7: Dreams and Mirages

p. 78   Quinn raises the possibility of an invitation in *SF* on page 216.

pp. 79–80   Quinn recounts the history of Grenville's men in *SF* on pages 151–54.

p. 81   For this grim description of Ireland, see Quinn, *RBE,* pages 130–31.

p. 82   On Ralegh's grant, see Quinn, *RBE,* page 136.

      Ralegh's boast is in Quinn, *RBE,* page 148.

      Lacey implies, on page 139, that Ralegh not only advocated for the potato but actually introduced it to Ireland.

p. 83   "When I found my self" from "The Excuse" in Latham, page 37.

      "Would God" from "A Poem Put into My Lady Laiton's Pocket by Sir W. Ralegh" in Latham, page 74.

p. 85   The gossip about Essex is quoted in Somerset, page 470.

      For Essex, see Lacey Baldwin Smith, *The Elizabethan Epic* (London: J. Cape, 1966). She is especially good at understanding these larger-than-life personalities; the quotation from Elizabeth is on page 219. The pages are described in Neale on page 321, and Essex's declaration to the queen is on page 322.

p. 86   For Marlowe's and Ralegh's entertaining poems, see Oakeshott, pages 34–35.

◼ ◼ ◼

Chapter 8: The New Hope and the Terrible Year

p. 87   Quinn explains White's motivations in *SF* on page 254.

p. 88   Quinn analyzes the White/Fernandez issue in *SF* and supplies the quotation on page 278. White suspected Fernandez of being an agent for the enemy who wanted to destroy the colony. Quinn sees this as unlikely.

p. 89   On Virginia Dare, see Quinn, *SF*, page 287.

p. 90   For Regiomontanus, see Garrett Mattingly, *The Defeat of the Spanish Armada* (London: J. Cape, 1959; reprint ed., Reprint Society, 1959), page 173. Mattingly is the great historian of the Armada, in part because his book is so readable. It is a treat for all readers. The translation from Latin is his.

pp. 90–91   This wonderful story can be found in Mattingly on page 175. Needless to say it was wishful thinking on the part of the Catholic spy.

p. 92   Mattingly describes the dedication of the fleet on page 207.

For Drake, see Mattingly, page 247.

p. 93   This revealing assessment is in Mattingly on pages 208–9. His sources do not reveal the name of the captain.

For types of ships, see Mattingly, page 205; for galleass, see page 236.

pp. 93–94   On the two kinds of war, see Mattingly, page 190.

p. 94   On the *Ark Ralegh*, see Lacey, page 128.

Lacey attributes the beacons to Ralegh on page 131; Mattingly gives this vivid description of the flares on page 258.

On the face of it the Spanish crescent is reminiscent of the deployment of troops used by Shaka Zulu in his land wars. It would be interesting to compare under what circumstances different military leaders have arrived at using such a strategy.

pp. 97–98   Mattingly tells the story of the night of the hellburners on pages 305–7.

p. 99   Lacey quotes Ralegh on page 132.

For the medal, see Lacey, page 132; Philip is quoted in Arthur Quinn, *A New World: An Epic of Colonial America from the Founding of Jamestown to the Fall of Quebec* (New York: Berkley, 1995), page 7. (There is no relationship between Arthur and David B. Quinn.)

Here is a perfect moment in parallel world history. When the Mongols sought to invade Japan in 1274 and again in 1281, their Korean-built ships were blasted by storms. In both Japan and England a *kamikaze*, a "divine wind," saved an island kingdom.

p. 101   For Elizabeth's speech, see Mattingly, page 329.

CHAPTER 9: THE AGONY OF JOHN WHITE

p. 102   For the date of this ban, see Quinn, *SF*, page 300.

Quinn tells of this aborted effort in *SF* on pages 301–2

p. 103   Quinn continues the story with this second effort in *SF* on pages 304–5,

pp. 104–5   Quinn tell of this Spanish piece of the lost colony puzzle in *SF* on pages 307–8.

p. 105   On the new financing, see Quinn, *SF*, pages 310–11.

For the makeup of the fleet and the last-minute changes, see Quinn, *SF*, page 318.

Any aspiring salvagers can find clues in Quinn, *SF*, on page 322.

p. 106   For the trumpet call, see Morison, page 675.

For White's words, see Quinn, *SF*, pages 326–27.

White's report on the word written on the tree continues in Quinn, *SF*, page 327.

p. 107   White's sad moment is in Quinn, *SF*, page 329.

pp. 108–9   Quinn recounts this bloody and tragic possible end to the lost colony in *SF* on pages 362–69.

p. 109   For the number and date of the last Hatteras, see Quinn, *SF*, page 377.

p. 110   For statistics on tobacco and Jamestown, see A. Quinn, *A New World*, page 35.

EL DORADO

p. 111   Shakespeare, *Measure for Measure*, Act I, Scene 2.

Chapter 10: The Lie

p. 113   "Gold," "Small drops," and "regal looks" are from Ralegh's "Ocean to Cynthia" in Oakeshott, in order on pages 179 and 178.

p. 114   Lacey quotes this anonymous letter on page 171.

"She is gone." "Alone," "flames," and "twelve years" all also from "Ocean" in Oakeshott, in order on pages 202, 181, 185, and 182.

p. 116   This version of "The Lie" can be found in Oakeshott, pages 52–54. There are many debates among scholars about this poem: Did Ralegh write it? Was it written by his enemies and falsely attributed to him to get him into trouble? If he did write it, when and why? Finally, whenever he wrote it, how should it be evaluated—as an intense expression of his personality or as a commonplace and minor work? Compared with some poems that are more surely Ralegh's, it does have a singsong sameness of both rhythm and emotion that can, depending on your point of view, contribute to its power or make it seem obvious. Several important and recent studies tend to see it as Ralegh's, and as a major work. Greenblatt summarizes the authorship debate in his appendix, pages 171–76. Whoever wrote it, and no matter how we judge its literary quality, it is a clear expression of one side of Ralegh's character and deserves to be read for that reason alone.

p. 117   For "truthless dreams" in "Farewell to the Court," see Oakeshott, page 170.

"Desire" is from "A Poesie to Prove Affection Is Not Love" in Latham, page 41.

p. 118   For Shakespeare's famous lines on acting, *As You Like It*, Act II, Scene 7.

p. 119   Hamlet's soliloquy comes in *Hamlet*, Act III, Scene 1.

p. 120   For Ralegh's note, see Lacey, page 170. The author of the report was his cousin, a poet named Sir Arthur Gorges.

On the *Madre de Dios*, see Lacey, page 174.

p. 121   For Ralegh on his ransom, see Lacey, page 176.

p. 122   Ralegh in Parliament can be found in Lacey, page 190.

p. 123   Ralegh and atheism is in Lacey, page 195.

The question of the relationship between Ralegh and his circle and *Love's Labour's Lost* is much debated. For a recent discussion of these issues, see the scholarly but informative introduction to the World's Classics edition of the play, written by G. R. Hibbard (Oxford: Oxford University Press, 1994).

pp. 123–24   The story of how Ralegh found out about El Dorado is told in many places, including Hemming, pages 160–61, 165; Lacey, pages 202–5. The famous essayist V. S. Naipaul, who grew up in Trinidad, went to orginal sources to research *The Loss of El Dorado: A History* (reprint ed.: Harmondsworth, England: Penguin, 1978), pages 30–31.

Chapter 11:
The Discovery of the Golden Kingdom

p. 125   Ralegh is quoted in Lacey on page 203; Lacey, like most others, calls this man Martinez; Hemming, who seems to have done the most research on him, uses the slightly different and longer form, see Hemming, pages 160–61; Naipaul calls him Albujar—see pages 30–31.

p. 127   Ralegh on the Empire of Guiana is from his *Discoverie*, as quoted in Nicholl on page 36.

p. 129   Ralegh quotes Berrío in *Discoverie* on page 35.

Ralegh on the Delta is in *Discoverie*, page 39; Nicholl, page 126, mentions the flag.

Nicholl looks at Ralegh's trip two ways: through what he experienced when he retraced Ralegh's journey up the Orinoco in 1995 and through reading as many relevant sources from Ralegh's time as he could find. This chapter owes a great deal to Nicholl, and I recommend *The Creature in the Map* highly to anyone who wants to know more about Ralegh, the search for El Dorado, this region of South America, or the literature of Ralegh's day. It is written for a general audience and many younger readers should not find it too hard. But it does assume some knowledge of literary criticism, or a willingness to see hidden feelings, motives, or attitudes in the words we choose and how we string them together. He has an excellent chapter on the implications of the Red Cross River, see pages 304–13.

For Ralegh's speech to the caciques, see *Discoverie*, page 7.

pp. 129–30   For Ralegh's insistence that natives be well treated, see *Discoverie*, page 52.

p. 131   For Ralegh's praise of the natives, see *Discoverie*, page 42.

Nicholl shows how he decided that the river Ralegh started out on was the Manomo on pages 129–31.

pp. 131–32   For Ralegh's story of these "we're just about there" promises, see *Discoverie*, page 45.

p. 132   His description of the birds is on the same page.

The story of the long journey to the Arawak village in *Discoverie*, pages 46–47.

p. 133   Ralegh's beautiful paragraph about the edenic scene is in *Discoverie*, page 48.

Both Nicholl, page 153, and an undated private communication from Maricel Presilla, a good friend who has traveled through this landscape, affirm the accuracy of Ralegh's description.

p. 134   For the alligator story see *Discoverie*, page 48; Nicholl pages 153–54.

p. 135   The story of the canoes and the Spanish refining equipment is in *Discoverie*, pages 49–50.

The women serving the men in the hammock can be found in *Discoverie*, page 55.

p. 137   For Topiawari's story, see *Discoverie*, page 63.

p. 139   Ralegh on the waterfalls is in *Discoverie*, page 67.

Ralegh's homage to the beautiful country is on the same page.

p. 141   Ralegh's wonderful summary is in *Discoverie*, page 96.

p. 142   To this day, we have not learned how to solve exactly the conflict Ralegh described. Though Ralegh was wrong about the Inca kingdom, he was right about the gold ore. There are great reserves of gold quite near where he looked for it. Should we exploit those reserves or preserve this verdant landscape? A Canadian company called Omai runs the biggest mining operation in this region. As part of its refining process this company uses cyanide. In 1995 a large pool holding cyanide-poisoned water broke, sending death down the rivers. As fish, birds, and animals died, Ralegh's virgin land was despoiled. If we want our own El Dorado, our land that produces gold, we have to use deadly poisons. If we want to preserve what is left of a virginal land, we will have to give up millions of dollars' worth of gold that can support many poor people in struggling countries such as Brazil, Guyana, and Venezuela. Which should we do?

CHAPTER 12: MY LORD OF ESSEX

pp. 141–50   The story of Cádiz, and of Ralegh and Essex, appears in every book on Ralegh, Elizabeth, and this period. The versions I found most helpful include Smith, pages 207–33; Neale, pages 317–76; Wallace, pages 123–71; Lacey, pages 224–33. For Essex's sense of mission, see R. B. Wernham, *The Return of the Armadas: The Last Years of the Elizabethan War Against Spain, 1595–1603* (Oxford, England: Clarendon Press, Oxford University Press, 1994), page 123. Though this study has much more day-to-day information on this period than any general reader could possibly want, it is also a treasure trove of stories and facts.

p. 145   For details of the Spanish attack, see Wernham, page 32. As an example of how useful this book is, none of the standard Ralegh biographies can agree on which village or villages the Spanish attacked, while Wernham goes to primary sources to name them.

Howard on Essex is quoted in Wernham, pages 55 and 90. Smith gives the consuming fire quote on page 222, but unfortunately she never lists her own sources.

pp. 145–46   Most accounts of Cádiz list 10,000 soldiers; Wernham refines this to planned forces of 5,000 soldiers and 5,000 marines on page 59, and comes to a final count of 6,000 for the army on page 83. He describes the gentlemen on the same page, and the flags on page 84. A footnote also on page 84 suggests that 120 is an undercount for the fleet.

p. 146   Howard's doctor is quoted in Lacey, page 228. For Ralegh on Grenville, see his "A Report of the Truth of the Fight About the Iles of Azores this Last Summer Betwixt the *Revenge,* one of Her Majesty's ships, and an Armada of the King of Spain" in Hyder E. Rollins and Herchel Baker, eds., *The Renaissance in England: Non-dramatic Prose and Verse of the Sixteenth Century* (Boston: Heath, 1954), page 897.

p. 147   Ralegh did not know about the glass story, which came from a Dutch resident of the Azores. See Wallace, page 88.

For Ralegh on revenge, see Lacey, page 229.

For one of the many wonderful accounts of Ralegh's great day at Cádiz, see Wallace, page 131.

p. 149   For Ralegh on this burning hell, see Wallace, pages 134–35.

p. 150   Wernham sets the crown's average intake as 350,000 Elizabethan pounds in note 7 on page 47, and the value of the fleet as 3,500,000 pounds on page 102; he summarizes and extends these calculations on page 121.

Wernham quotes this contemporary praise of the victory on page 107.

CHAPTER 13: MISCHIEVOUS MATCHIVEL

p. 152   Wernham quotes Bacon on pages 133–34.

Smith quotes Burghley's advice to Cecil on page 231, but does not cite her own source.

p. 154   Wernham quotes Essex on Spanish gold on page 126.

pp. 154–55   For the story of Ralegh's mad bravery at Fayal, see Smith, page 229. Once again she gives no source for the quote on the Spanish marksmen.

p. 155   Wernham recounts the little-known (in America) but fascinating second act of the Armada story on pages 184–85.

p. 156   Wernham quotes Essex's late resolve on page 188.

Wernham quotes Essex's despair on page 313 and the account of his entrance on page 317.

p. 157   Smith quotes Essex's disdain of the aged Elizabeth on page 74.

Lacey quotes Ralegh's warning letter to Cecil on page 262.

p. 158   For Elizabeth on *Richard II,* see Lacey page 265.

This ballad can be found in Wallace on page 173.

p. 159   Howard's hatred of Ralegh is quoted in Lacey on page 274.

p. 160   For Elizabeth's Golden Speech, see Neale, pages 384–85; Somerset, page 551, gives the political context.

CHAPTER 14: THE PLAY OF TREASON

pp. 161–62   For James's pun, see Wallace, page 190. On the tobacco conflict, see Alvin Kernan, *Shakespeare, the King's Playwright: Theater in the Stuart Court* (New Haven: Yale

University Press, 1995), page 55. This is a study for specialists but is a treat for Shakespeare fans.

p. 164   The run up to Ralegh's treason trial, including the question of what he may or may not have been been guilty of, is in all the standard biographies. For the possible implications of the transfer of Ralegh's estate, see Lacey, pages 287–88.

p. 165   For Shakespeare's line on bait, *Hamlet,* Act II, Scene 1.

p. 166   For Ralegh's jailer, see Wallace, page 196.

For Cecil on Ralegh's suicide attempt, see Greenblatt, pages 114–15.

p. 167   For Ralegh's suicide note, see Greenblatt, page 115.

p. 168   For this damning picture of treason law in Ralegh's time, see John Macdonell, *Historical Trials* (Oxford: Clarendon Press, Oxford University Press, 1927), page 192.

p. 169   Wallace, page 202, gives the context of Ralegh's trip to the trial; Lacey, page 295, quotes the jailer.

For "spider," see Catherine Drinker Bowen, *The Lion and the Throne: The Life and Times of Sir Edward Coke* (Boston: Little, Brown, 1957), page 207. This biography of Coke has a detailed, quotation-filled, engaging account of the trial.

For Ralegh and Coke's first exchange, see Lacey, page 298.

p. 170   For "Lady," see Bowen, page 199.

For Ralegh's response to the Spanish accusation, see Greenblatt, page 118.

For Ralegh's grand speech on judgment, see Greenblatt, pages 118–19.

p. 171   For Ralegh and Coke's battle over the last word, see Greenblatt, pages 119–20.

For Judge Popham's verdict, see Bowen, page 217.

p. 172   For the first admiring observer, see Greenblatt, page 116; for the second, see Wallace, page 217.

For James's spy, see Wallace, page 217.

p. 173   For the story of the mock execution, see Kernan, pages 57–58.

p. 174   For the seating arrangements at the first royal performance of *Hamlet,* see Kernan, page 32.

Hamlet's plan concludes the second and final scene of the second act.

The analysis of *Measure for Measure* and its link to the Ralegh trial is taken from Kernan, pages 59–68.

Chapter 15: The Story of Our Days

p. 177   For Ralegh's dedication of his History to Henry, see Wallace, page 243.

p. 179   For Ralegh on human and divine causation, see C. A. Patrides, ed., intro., *The History of the World* (Philadelphia: Temple Univesity Press, 1971), page 157. Patrides's introduction to the history is an excellent guide to Ralegh, his book, and his times.

Hamlet on divine and human causation comes in Act V, scene 2.

Henry on Ralegh and James can be found in Lacey, page 324.

p. 180   For a fuller account of the reasons for James's poverty and the sequence of trips to South America, see Lacey, pages 332–38.

p. 183   For Ralegh to his wife, see Latham, page 10 (brains), and Lacey, page 359 (providence).

p. 184   For Ralegh's rewritten final poem, see Oakeshott, page 209.

pp. 184–85   For the story of Ralegh's death, see Wallace, pages 315–16.

p. 186   For the ending quote, see William Carlos Williams, *In the American Grain* (New York: Albert & Charles Boni, 1921), page 62.

Time Line

YEAR	RALEGH	ENGLAND / EUROPE
1455		Gutenberg prints first Bible with movable type
1492		
1509		Henry VIII becomes king of England and marries Catherine of Aragon
1512		
1516		Mary I born
1517		Luther posts his theses at Wittenberg
1521		
1527		Henry questions legality of his marriage
1532		
1533		Henry marries Anne Boleyn Elizabeth I born
1534		Henry becomes supreme head of the Church of England
1536		First English monasteries dissolved English translation of the Bible in churches Anne Boleyn executed for adultery; Henry marries Jane Seymour
1537		Edward VI born; Jane Seymour dies
1537–8		
1539		All English monasteries taken by the Crown
1540		Henry marries Catherine Howard
1542		Catherine Howard executed for adultery Mary, Queen of Scots, born
1543		
1547		Henry dies, Edward becomes king Use of English in churches made mandatory
1553		Edward dies, Mary becomes queen All Edward's laws on religion annulled
1554	Ralegh born	Elizabeth sent to the Tower Mary marries Philip II of Spain

ARTS/SCIENCES	NEW WORLD / ASIA
	COLUMBUS ARRIVES IN NEW WORLD
MICHELANGELO COMPLETES SISTINE CHAPEL CEILING	
THOMAS MORE'S *UTOPIA* PUBLISHED	
	HERNANDO CORTÉS CONQUERS AZTEC EMPIRE
NICCOLÒ MACHIAVELLI'S *THE PRINCE* PUBLISHED	
	FRANCISCO PIZARRO CONQUERS INCA EMPIRE
	GONZALO JIMÉNEZ DE QUESADA CONQUERS CHIBCHA
	FIRST EUROPEANS EXPLORE AREA NEAR THE ORINOCO
NICOLAUS COPERNICUS'S MAJOR WORK PUBLISHED	

YEAR	RALEGH	ENGLAND / EUROPE
1558		MARY DIES, ELIZABETH BECOMES QUEEN
1559		PROTESTANTISM MADE THE ESTABLISHED RELIGION IN ENGLAND
1561		
1564		
1566		JAMES I BORN
1568	RALEGH AT OXFORD	
1569	RALEGH FIGHTING IN FRANCE	
1571		BATTLE OF LEPANTO; NAVAL POWER OF OTTOMAN TURKS IS BROKEN
1572		ST. BARTHOLOMEW'S DAY MASSACRE IN FRANCE
1575	RALEGH BACK IN ENGLAND, TRAINING AS LAWYER	
1578	GILBERT, WITH RALEGH, SETS OUT TO ENFORCE PATENT TO SETTLE NEW WORLD	ELIZABETH GOES ON PROGRESS TO NORWICH
1579		CHRISTOPHER SAXTON PUBLISHES FIRST ATLAS OF MAPS OF ENGLAND
1580	RALEGH PARTICIPATES IN MASSACRE IN IRELAND	
1582	RALEGH NAMED ONE OF THREE IN CHARGE OF MUNSTER IN IRELAND	
1583	RALEGH GAINS RIGHT TO RENT DURHAM HOUSE	
1584	RALEGH GAINS PATENT TO SETTLE NEW WORLD; KNIGHTED; IN PARLIAMENT	ROBERT DEVEREUX, EARL OF ESSEX, APPEARS AT COURT
1585		
1586		
1587	RALEGH GAINS CONTROL OF HUGE AREAS OF CORK AND WATERFORD IN IRELAND RALEGH APPOINTED CAPTAIN OF THE QUEEN'S GUARD	MARY, QUEEN OF SCOTS, EXECUTED
1588		SPANISH ARMADA
1590		
1591		

ARTS / SCIENCES	NEW WORLD / ASIA
GORBODUC, FIRST ENGLISH TRAGEDY WILLIAM SHAKESPEARE BORN	
	SIR FRANCIS DRAKE CAPTURES PANAMA, ATTACKS AND RAIDS SPANISH HOLDINGS
	GILBERT, WITH RALEGH, SETS OUT TO ENFORCE PATENT TO SETTLE NEW WORLD DRAKE CLAIMS SAN FRANCISCO BAY REGION AS NEW ALBION
	GILBERT DISAPPEARS AT SEA FIRST EXPEDITION TO ROANOKE (AMADAS AND BARLOWE)
	SECOND EXPEDITION TO ROANOKE (GRENVILLE, LANE, HARIOT, WHITE) ANTONIO DE BERRÍO SEARCHES ORINOCO FOR EL DORADO LANE'S GROUP RETURNED TO ENGLAND BY DRAKE; SOME MEN LEFT BEHIND? GRENVILLE LEAVES 15 MEN ON ROANOKE THIRD EXPEDITION TO ROANOKE (LOST COLONY) WHITE RETURNS TO ENGLAND
SHAKESPEARE'S *HENRY VI* WRITTEN	WHITE PREVENTED FROM LEAVING ENGLAND; ATTACKED BY PIRATES ON SECOND ATTEMPT BERRÍO COMPLETES THREE-YEAR SEARCH OF ORINOCO WHITE SAILS TO AMERICA, BUT LEAVES, NEVER TO GO BACK BERRÍO RETURNS FROM THIRD TRIP ALONG ORINOCO

YEAR	RALEGH	ENGLAND / EUROPE
1592	RALEGH GETS ELIZABETH THROCKMORTON PREGNANT, MARRIES HER RALEGH AND WIFE IMPRISONED IN DURHAM HOUSE, TOWER OF LONDON, THEN FREED "OCEAN TO CYNTHIA" WRITTEN?	*MADRE DE DIOS* BROUGHT TO ENGLAND
1593	RALEGH FAVORS RELIGIOUS TOLERATION IN PARLIAMENT	
1594	RALEGH CHARGED WITH ATHEISM, ACQUITTED	
1595	RALEGH GOES IN SEARCH OF EL DORADO, CAPTURES BERRÍO	
1596	RALEGH PUBLISHES *THE DISCOVERY OF GUIANA*	RALEGH, ESSEX, CHARLES HOWARD ATTACK CÁDIZ
1597	RALEGH REAPPOINTED CAPTAIN OF THE GUARD	RALEGH, ESSEX, THOMAS HOWARD FAIL IN ATTACK ON AZORES
1598		
1599		ESSEX FAILS IN IRELAND, SIGNS ILLEGAL TREATY
1600		
1601		ESSEX SEES *RICHARD II*, REBELS, FAILS, EXECUTED ELIZABETH'S GOLDEN SPEECH
1602	RALEGH SELLS LAST HOLDINGS IN IRELAND	
1603	RALEGH ARRESTED, CONVICTED OF TREASON, SENT TO TOWER	ELIZABETH DIES; JAMES BECOMES KING OF ENGLAND
1604		
1605		
1607		
1608	RALEGH BECOMES TUTOR TO PRINCE HENRY	
1612		HENRY DIES
1613	RALEGH'S *HISTORY OF THE WORLD* PUBLISHED	
1616	RALEGH FREED FROM TOWER	
1617	RALEGH, WAT RALEGH, LAWRENCE KEYMIS SAIL FOR EL DORADO WAT KILLED, KEYMIS SUICIDE	
1618	RALEGH EXECUTED	

ARTS / SCIENCES	NEW WORLD / ASIA
	RALEGH GOES IN SEARCH OF EL DORADO; CAPTURES BERRÍO
EDMUND SPENSER'S *FAERIE QUEEN* PUBLISHED	
LOVE'S LABOUR'S LOST PUBLISHED, PERHAPS ABOUT RALEGH	
	BRITISH EAST INDIA COMPANY FORMED (FROM 1753 TO 1948 ENGLISH RULE INDIA)
HAMLET PERFORMED FOR THE KING	
MEASURE FOR MEASURE WRITTEN AND PERFORMED, ABOUT RALEGH TRIAL?	
MIGUEL DE CERVANTES'S *DON QUIXOTES, PART I*, PUBLISHED	
	JAMESTOWN COLONY
SHAKESPEARE DIES	
	RALEGH, WAT RALEGH, LAWRENCE KEYMIS SAIL FOR EL DORADO

Index

Note: Page numbers in *italic* type refer to illustrations.